Allen Wallace

YOUR CHILD

AND

INVESTMENT

Young

And

Invested

Copyright© 2021 Allen Wallace

All Rights Reserved.

Table Of Contents

INTRODUCTION

HOW TO INVEST IN YOUR CHILDREN AND TEACH SELF-SUFFICIENCY TO THEM

CHAPTER ONE

THE BEST INVESTMENTS FOR CHILDREN

Options for a Child Investment Account: Taxable

1. Custodial Accounts

Options For Tax-Advantaged Child Investment Accounts

2. 529 Savings Plans

Plans for College Savings

Plans for Prepaid Tuition

3. Traditional and Roth Individual Retirement Accounts

How To Put In Place A Custodial IRA In Your Child's Name

4. Education Savings Account (Coverdell).

CHAPTER TWO

CHILDREN'S INVESTMENTS

1. Stocks

2. Exchange-Traded Funds (ETFs)

3. Investing in Mutual Funds

4. Account for Savings

Where Can Grandchildren Open Investment and Bank Accounts?

CHAPTER THREE

OTHER ASSETS TO GIVE YOUR CHILDREN

There are savings bonds

Money

How to Give Stock as a Gift

• Taxes on Capital Gains

• Gift Tax Regulations

• Financial Control

CHAPTER FOUR

INVESTING FOR A CHILD'S FUTURE

Best children Money Apps (Debit Cards, Investing & Mgmt)

Making Your Own Spending Decisions

Is It Possible To Get A Debit Card For My Child?

Greenlight Card (Investment Account with Debit Card).

CHAPTER FIVE

OTHER EXCELLENT INVESTMENT APPS FOR CHILDREN

Acorns (bonus of $10)

Greenlight

EarlyBird ($10 Bonus)

Stash ($5 Bonus)

M1 Finance (bonus of $30)

UNest ($25 Bonus)

CHAPTER SIX

CHILDREN'S ALLOWANCE APPS

Rooster Money

Savings Spree

PiggyBot.

iAllowance.

CHAPTER SEVEN

EVERYTHING YOU NEED TO KNOW ABOUT DEBIT CARDS AND CHILDREN

What Is A Children's Debit Card?

Is It Possible To Get A Debit Card For A Child Under The Age Of 13?

Which Debit Cards Are Best For Kids And Teens?

Best Rated Overall

The Best Free Debit Card For Children And Adolescents

The Best For Customer Service

The Best For Value

Axos Bank First Checking Debit Card for Teens

Famzoo Is The Best For Financial Education

Acorns are the best for long-term growth

Current: The Best For Product Features And Innovation.

Stash Is The Best Option When Approaching Finances For The First Time.

Roostermoney: The Best App For Handling Allowances.

M1 Finance Is The Best For Financial Automation.

Jassby Virtual Debit Card For Kids.

Honorable Mention: Nationwide Bank First Checking Offers A Free Teen Debit Card.

CHAPTER EIGHT

FEATURES TO LOOK FOR IN KIDS AND TEENS DEBIT CARDS

1. Making A Direct Deposit
2. Checking Account
3. Savings Account
4. Instant Money Transfer
5. Use Of The Mobile App
6. No Overdraft Fees
7. Reasonably Priced Monthly Fees
8. Parental Controls
9. Kids' Reloadable Prepaid Debit Cards
10. There Is No Minimum Balance Requirement
11. Money Management Features
12. Interest Paid By The Parents
13. Set Savings Objectives
14. Establish Spending Boundaries
15. Have Control Over How Your Children Spend Money On The Internet
16. Tools For Financial Literacy
17. Fee-Free ATM Withdrawals Online-Only Banks Faced An Early Challenge:
18. Rewarding Schemes
19. Round Ups
20. Ability To Make Charitable Contributions

21. Parental And Adolescent Safety

22. FDIC Coverage

23. Oversees Chores And Distributes Allowances

24. Investing Alternatives For Compounding Returns

CHAPTER NINE

FINANCIAL LESSONS DEBIT CARDS FOR CHILDREN TEACH

CHAPTER TEN

DEBIT CARDS FOR KIDS VS. PREPAID CARDS FOR KIDS

Is It OK For Kids To Use Prepaid Cards?

What To Do Before Getting A Debit Card For Kids

Can An 8-Year-Old, 11-Year-Old, 12-Year-Old, Or 16-Year-Old Have A Prepaid Debit Card?

Are Kids Too Young For Debit Cards?

Is A Kids' Debit Card A Good Option For Teens?

Are Children's Debit Cards Safe?

Do Kids' And Teens' Debit Cards Collect Personal Information?

What Are Some Other Investment Accounts For Kids That I Should Look Into?

Should Children Handle Money?

What Happens If My Child's Debit Card Is Stolen?

Is It Possible For Kids To Get Their Own (Custom) Debit Cards?

What Documents Are Required To Open A Debit Card For Children And Teenagers?

Is It Possible To Make Contactless Payments With A Teen Debit Card?

CHAPTER ELEVEN

CONCLUSION

When Opening A Brokerage Account For Your Child, These Are The Things To Look For

Choose An Account Type

Select The Appropriate Broker

Open The Account

Assist Your Child In Deciding What To Buy

INTRODUCTION

I can't tell you how many hours I devoted to reading, researching, and watching films about the best programs for investing in children's futures and the best investments for children. It's simple to feel overwhelmed when there are so many options available.

For nearly anything these days, including investing for your children, you can find a website or app dedicated to investments.

The difficulty is that not all websites are created equal; some may be better than others in terms of giving factual information on a given topic.

I wrote this book about the best investments for kids and child investing programs to consider for your own children because of this. Its objective is to expose you to the most modern options as a parent or grandparent. Depending on their unique situation, you can be explicit about which investments are best for your child's needs.

Let's get this party started!

HOW TO INVEST IN YOUR CHILDREN AND TEACH SELF-SUFFICIENCY TO THEM

Investing for children is simple if you know where to begin. Parents are frequently concerned about providing for their children as they get older and moving them to make their own financial decisions.

Teaching children about money and allowing them to begin investing while they are still minors should help to alleviate this fear.

And you don't have to come from a wealthy family to have a secure financial future. There's no need to come into the world with a silver spoon if you have spirit and perseverance.

You should not only focus on teaching your children financial literacy, but you should also demonstrate how making these decisions on a regular basis will play a key role in their lives.

Here are the fast sets of measures for parents who want to get their kids on the correct financial road as soon as possible:

- Begin investing in your children's future and showing them how to participate by teaching them about money, its value, and how to earn it.

- Increase your children's earning potential by teaching and practicing soft qualities such as collaboration, compassion, and teamwork, as well as encouraging schooling and extracurricular activities.

- Show children how to put these talents together to create a profession and invest their earnings for a secure financial future.

Let's look at some of the greatest investments for kids and child investment programs to consider for getting your child started now that you've completed these steps.

CHAPTER ONE

THE BEST INVESTMENTS FOR CHILDREN

Options for a Child Investment Account: Taxable

1. Custodial Accounts

Custodial accounts, also known as the Uniform Gifts to Minors Act (UGMA) and the Uniform Transfers to Minors Act (UTMA), allow you to place money into a specific account for a minor child or grandchild.

You have control of the account as the custodian or trustee until your child reaches adulthood, which is normally 18 to 21 years old. When your child reaches adulthood, he or she becomes the owner of their own account and is free to do whatever they choose with the money. This implies they are free to spend the money on whatever they wish.

Parents, grandparents, and other loved ones, on the other hand, can make significant contributions to these custodial accounts without triggering the gift tax by giving up to $15,000 per year per individual ($30,000 per married couple).

If you're worried about your child's assets affecting their eligibility for federal financial aid, a custodial account might not be the best option.

Students are required to contribute a bigger percentage of their savings than their parents, typically 20% vs. 5.6 percent for parents.

The illustrations below indicate the ideal custodial accounts to think about while starting a taxable account. You can also open a custodial IRA with M1 Finance, which will be detailed later in this book.

These designs indicate ratings (out of five), fees, what it's best for, and special offers:

Acorns Early: The Acorn Round-Ups $10 sign up bonus when making a first deposit at account opening, early 4.8 rating, $1/month - $5/month, automatic investing in the background into varied investments; Round-Ups $10 sign up bonus when making a first deposit at account opening.

Greenlight + Invest: (4.8 rating, $7.98/month) teaches investing concepts with parental guidance; allows individual and index fund investing; first month is free.

EarlyBird: 4.0 rating, $1/month if over $200 invested; $2/gift paid by gifter, simple gifting and saving in a UGMA account for affordable costs, $10 for account opening.

Stash: ($1/month - $9/month), 4.7 rating, regular folks looking to start managing their finances, For a deposit of $5 or more, you will receive a $5 stock bonus.

M1 Finance: Fee-free active trading and automated investing, Custodial IRAs, 4.3 rating, $0 trading or automated investing; $125/year on M1 Plus subscription for custodial account, fee-free active trading and automated investing. With a $1,000 deposit, you'll get a $30 welcome incentive.

UNest: 4.5 rating, $3-$6 per month, age-based contributions in a custodial investment account, matching bonus with a $25 initial deposit ($25 incentive).

Options For Tax-Advantaged Child Investment Accounts

2. 529 Savings Plans
College and Qualified Education Expenses Can Be Saved Tax-Free A 529 plan is a special tax-advantaged

investment plan that allows families to save for a beneficiary's current and future educational costs.

Previously, these plans could only pay qualified educational expenses for college students, but tax legislation in 2018 expanded the scope to include eligible spending for K-12 students as well.

Consider a 529 savings plan as one of the greatest ways to invest $1,000 or more each year for a child. When you liquidate the investments in the account, you can support your child financially while lowering your personal tax liability.

The amount you and others can contribute to a child's 529 Plan is restricted. Contributions are made after-tax, so you won't be able to deduct them.

If the funds go toward qualified educational expenses, the contributions grow tax-free from federal income tax, just like a Roth account. The majority of states also allow tax-free withdrawals.

Each year, you can donate up to the annual federal gift tax exclusion amount, which in 2021 is $15,000 per person ($30,000 for married couples filing jointly).

This "annual exclusion" indicates the maximum amount you can transfer as a gift to each person without incurring a gift tax, just like with custodial accounts.

If you have the ability, consider "superfunding" your child's 529 plan by making a five-year gift per child per person. This allows you to give a large sum of money without having to pay the gift tax.

Understandably, not every parent can afford such a large commitment, especially if they have numerous children ($150,000 per child if both parents contribute) who need to pay for college.

However, if possible, this allows the money to compound over several years, starting when your children are little.

You might want to approach your parents for assistance with their grandchildren. This is without a doubt one of the best investments you can make for your grandchildren.

However, because this option has a lot of rules, you need seek the advice of a tax specialist if you want to make these payments successfully.

In addition, 529 plans just received approval to improve how you can use the assets in your account (i.e., without incurring the 10 percent withdrawal penalty).

The SECURE Act is a package of laws aimed at helping people plan for their retirement and save more money.

According to the new law, up to $10,000 per year in 529 savings plans can be used to pay down student loan debt or expenses associated with registered apprenticeship programs.

There are two types of 529 plans:

Plans for College Savings
Traditional 401(k) s and IRAs work similarly to College Savings Plans. Your contributions are invested in mutual funds or other investment vehicles, such as target date funds, which are age-based investments.

However, these goals differ slightly from those of age-based funds seen in retirement plans. As your child approaches college age, instead of gradually becoming more conservative as you approach retirement, they transfer to more solid underlying investments.

Unlike retirement programs, these schemes are also administered at the state level.

Backer is one company to consider when it comes to starting a 529 College Savings Plan. The organization offers top-tier 529 Savings Plans that allow you to save for presents from family and friends via social savings.

For birthdays, holidays, or other important events (like making honor roll!), you can send an invite code for friends and family to make contributions to a 529 Savings Plan. Backer allows you to invest your school savings in a 529 plan tax-free while also allowing family and friends to contribute to your savings.

Plans for Prepaid Tuition

There is a way for parents of college-bound children to save money on their tuition, albeit it is not available in every state. Children can lock in today's tuition rates for the next 18 years and avoid paying rises over time by investing in a prepaid plan.

Prepaid tuition plans are essentially a college tuition presale that may be used as an alternative to saving for education.

The tuition scheme will pay for eligible beneficiaries' college expenditures while they are enrolled in school and then reimburse the participating institutions. You can transfer the value or seek for a refund if your child ends up attending a school outside of the state or a private institution.

3. Traditional and Roth Individual Retirement Accounts

An Individual Retirement Account, or IRA, is a tax-advantaged savings account in which you can keep stocks, ETFs, bonds, and other asset kinds. Young adults are the most common users of these accounts because they need the account owner to have a source of income. However, if your child starts earning a regular income, it may be good for them to form a custodial IRA in order to teach them about responsible money management and tax-efficient investing.

Then you may assist your children in selecting the greatest tax-advantaged investments from the time they are little children until adulthood.

You can make a contribution from your IRA to their educational expenditures. While you don't have to start taking required minimum distributions (RMDs) until you're 72, you can start as soon as you're 59.

In fact, if necessary, you can begin earlier. If the funds go toward paying for qualified higher education expenditures for yourself, your spouse, your children, or grandkids in the year you make the withdrawal, you can take money from your regular or Roth IRA without paying a 10% extra tax.

Withdrawing funds from an IRA before the age of 59½ avoids the 10% penalty, and while you will still have to pay income tax in most situations, having this cash on hand could be useful.

Using these funds to fund your child's or grandchild's college education, however, has its own set of disadvantages:

1. You deplete your retirement assets, and you won't be able to contribute again until you continue to work, so make sure you're well-funded outside of the IRA.

2. Withdrawing funds from a retirement account to pay for qualifying school expenses could jeopardize your eligibility for need-based financial aid the following year.

You might be able to set up a Roth IRA in your child's name if you don't want to dig into your retirement resources. This, however, comes with a caveat.

Specifically, throughout the contribution year, your child (not you) must have earned revenue from a job.

As long as they earn enough money, parents with the means can give up to the maximum annual contribution. The IRS doesn't mind where the money comes from as long as it doesn't exceed your child's annual earnings.

For example, if your child works as a waiter during the summer and earns $2,500, you can let them keep the money while you contribute to their Roth IRA.

That way, your child can do something else with their earnings while you put money into their retirement account in the same amount.

Remember that children must have earned income in order for anyone to contribute to their custodial IRA.

How To Put In Place A Custodial IRA In Your Child's Name

If you want to start a custodial IRA for your child, the account's custodian (that's you!) is responsible for managing and controlling the account's assets until the account's termination age, which is defined by state law. At this time, the assets and account are transferred to them.

Work with them while they're still young and looking for ways to get involved in teen investing. As a technique of teaching kids about money management, this can provide useful knowledge and direction.

You can utilize this to assist them in beginning long-term financial planning.

Here's how to go about it: Many of the best stock trading apps for beginners will let you set up a custodial IRA if your child is a minor (under 18 or 21 years old, depending on your state of residency).

M1 Finance, for example, allows you to open a custodial IRA by signing up for their M1 Plus subscription. The company provides this as a free service for the first year. After that, it's $125 per year.

Using this program to create a kid investing plan, you may automate investments for your child's future. The software can also help you diversify your portfolio by recommending index funds and companies.

Consider forming a custodial IRA with M1 Finance, and the app will even make a $30 contribution to help you get started if you deposit at least $1,000.

These can be used as free stocks to help your children's investment portfolios get off to a faster start.

- M1 Finance's Smart Money Management allows you the freedom and flexibility to invest, borrow, and spend your money automatically, with high-yield checking and cheap borrowing rates accessible.

- Special Offers: Open an account and make a $1,000 deposit within 14 days to receive a $30 bonus and a free year of M1 Plus ($125 value) through September 2021.

4. Education Savings Account (Coverdell).

A Coverdell Education Savings Account is a good way to save for college expenses.

Due to their favorable federal income tax status, Coverdell ESAs, like 529 plans, are one of the most popular school savings investment options.

In addition to college fees, these accounts allow you to put money toward eligible education expenses for K-12 grade schools.

If you utilize money from an ESA plan for nonqualified purposes, you will be charged a 10% penalty, much like with 529 Plans.

Furthermore, any gains realized in the account at the time of sale will be subject to capital gains tax.

Coverdell payments are not deductible and must be made before your children reach the age of 18. Or later if the Internal Revenue Service determines that they are a beneficiary with exceptional needs. You can set up multiple ESAs for a single beneficiary, but the maximum contribution is the same for all of them rather than a $2,000 limit for each on..

You can have many ESAs, but you can only contribute a total of $2,000 per year to all of them.

CHAPTER TWO

CHILDREN'S INVESTMENTS

1. Stocks

Stocks are one of the greatest investments for kids because they have a long-term focus and will give your children with years of profitable returns.

Individual equities, exchange-traded funds, and mutual funds are all options for holding stocks in the above-mentioned kid investment programs.

Whether it's a taxable account or a custodial IRA, custodial accounts allow you to hold a variety of assets in your child's name. Investing in equities for your children is a popular reason for opening a custodial account.

If you want to start investing on behalf of the child, you can open a custodial brokerage account.

Investing in the future of your children is a worthwhile and helpful activity. Stocks may be used to teach your children about the necessity of saving money, investing, and general money management skills.

To begin establishing an interest in investing, you may need to reach out to them in other aspects of their lives.

Consider developing an individual portfolio of stocks for youngsters they're likely to recognize from their daily life to get a child interested in the stock market.

Apple, Google, Disney, and a slew of other companies might be involved. If you invest in a portfolio of high-performing companies, your children's investment accounts will grow consistently over time.

These custodial accounts provide a slight tax benefit in the form of investment income tax breaks, while you must still pay taxes beyond certain thresholds due to the Kiddie Tax.

Parents must pay the marginal income tax rate on all unearned income realized in the account under this tax. For children under the age of 19 or full-time students under the age of 23, this regulation applies to all unearned income.

This does not result in the youngster paying higher taxes than they do now. The IRS allows the first $1,100 of unearned income to be tax-free, the next $1,100 to be taxed at the child's rate, and any remaining money to be taxed at the parents' rate.

This implies that if you put $1,000 into a custodial account for your child each year and they earn less than $1,100 in dividends, they are tax-free. If it's $1,600, though, you'll have to pay taxes on $500 of it.

If the account has $2,300 in dividends, $1,100 will be taxed at the child's rate, $1,100 at the parents' rate, and $100 will be taxed at the parents' rate.

If your child sells any of the stocks in their account later, they will have to pay capital gains tax. If held for more than a year, the gains may be subject to long-term capital gains tax rather than short-term capital gains tax, which may result in some tax savings.

Long-term capital gains tax rates are often lower, whereas short-term capital gains tax rates are the same as those applied to ordinary income.

2. Exchange-Traded Funds (ETFs)

Exchange-Traded Funds (ETFs) are a type of mutual fund that is traded on (ETFs)

Over the last two decades, ETFs have grown in popularity. By owning an underlying, diversified portfolio of stocks, bonds, and other investments, these investment vehicles mimic mutual fund performance.

They do, however, differ significantly in terms of openly trading on stock exchanges.

They frequently have better liquidity than mutual funds due to this aspect, as they trade throughout the day.

ETFs can be used to invest in both passive and active strategies. Passive ETFs are index funds that monitor the overall market and can also be tailored to a specific sector or group of assets.

Investing in index funds gives instant diversification in a single, low-cost investment. You don't have to pick stocks or engage in risky conduct like investing in order to get quick money.

Because passive ETFs invest in publicly listed companies or funds that aim to mirror the performance of a segment of the market, management costs are minimal.

They don't actively pick stocks or hire a research team to provide top stock research services in the hopes of outperforming the market.

Furthermore, trading commissions only apply if you don't use a free stock trading software.

Because they actively trade in and out of securities to achieve a declared investing objective, active ETFs can incur substantially higher management fees.

ETFs can pay dividends, which is a fantastic source of passive income to consider when putting together an income portfolio. They can also be used as long-term investments.

3. Investing in Mutual Funds

Although investing can be intimidating for anybody, many experts believe that young investors benefit from opening mutual fund accounts at a young age.

These investment vehicles, like ETFs, buy a basket of securities in order to achieve a certain investing goal.

Mutual funds pool your money with that of other investors to create portfolios of underlying investments. This results in a portfolio, which is a broader collection of stocks, bonds, and other investments.

When the value of a mutual fund's securities changes, the net asset value (NAV) is updated to reflect the change by calculating how much more—or less—the fund would have to sell its investments for to meet shareholder redemptions.

This price fluctuates dependent on the value of your portfolio's securities at the end of each market trading day.

The mere fact that an investor owns a mutual fund does not imply that the investor owns the underlying securities. They are the sole owners of the mutual fund shares.

There are two sorts of mutual funds: passively managed and actively managed mutual funds.

Active mutual fund managers make investment decisions based on their stock research and the fund's investment plan. The purpose of portfolio management is to outperform a comparable benchmark, which is a common but hazardous strategy.

Passively managed mutual funds aim to replicate the performance of a benchmark index such as the S&P 500, Dow Jones Industrial Average, or Barclays Corporate Bond Index.

You can invest in mutual funds for your children through IRAs, 529 Plans, and ESAs, allowing them to benefit from compounding returns in a diversified investment over time.

4. Account for Savings

Starting to save might be intimidating, but parents can combat this by making it a simple activity for their children through repetition and comprehension.

If you've already mastered the art of saving, be the parent who teaches your children the value of starting a savings account and forming excellent money habits as soon as feasible.

If you want to help your children develop a savings account balance or even open an account for them using a banking app for minors to manage money from their allowance or a part-time job, you have several alternatives.

They will be able to earn interest on their savings account while also learning how to bank as a result of this. Many even include debit cards for children and teenagers, allowing parents to keep track of spending and set spending limits.

You should consider the following factors while selecting a youth savings account:

- Interest rate

- Any fees or minimum balance restrictions

- The grandchild's ability to access the funds

- And the account's ability to grow with them as they age.

Where Can Grandchildren Open Investment and Bank Accounts?

You may want to think about which investment options to choose now that you know more about the different types of child investment plans and accounts available for you to open on behalf of your children.

Thankfully, there is a variety of all-in-one money apps for kids that allow them to begin saving, learn about spending, and invest for the first time.

Custodial IRAs are best with M1 Finance ($30 bonus).

M1 Finance is a one-stop shop for personal finance, allowing new investors to open an account in seconds.

You'll need to apply for an M1 Plus subscription, which costs $125 for a custodial account, if you want to use this as a kid's investment app. The company is offering a limited-time deal of a free first year (valued at $125).

Investors can use the program to generate Portfolio Pies, which are diverse portfolios that rebalance to help you meet your financial goals.

M1 Finance is a service that provides flexible, adjustable, and automated financial solutions to self-directed investors. The platform intelligently manages your money according to your preferences.

Consider opening a custodial account or a custodial IRA with M1 Finance today.

Greenlight App.

The Greenlight App is a mobile application that allows trading at $7.98 per month after a free one-month trial.

Greenlight + Invest is a kids' investment account that also includes a debit card.

It's simple to use and can be used as both a savings account and a banking app for teenagers. The app will cover the fundamentals of investing, such as how to invest in stocks and ETFs.

Because it necessitates connected accounts from the custodians' banks or brokerages, it works best if parents and/or grandparents are involved in the process.

With real money, real stocks, and real-life courses, the all-in-one package teaches them critical financial skills including money management and investment concepts.

You can use the investing feature to:

• Buy fractional shares of firms your children admire (kid-friendly equities)

• Begin investing with as little as $1 in your account (with fractional shares)

• No trading commissions beyond the monthly subscription price

• Every trade on individual stocks and ETFs with a market value of $1 billion or more must be approved by parents directly in the app.

Consider opening a Greenlight Card + Invest account for your children today to begin investing in a custodial brokerage account. The first month is free to test the product and determine whether it satisfies your demands for one of the best investments for children.

• Greenlight provides configurable parental restrictions for each child as well as real-time transaction notifications.

• Greenlight is the only debit card that allows you to specify which stores your children can use the card at.

- Through Greenlight Max, parents can use this app to show their children how to invest using a custodial account.

Acorns Early ($10 Bonus)

Acorns Prices: Acorns Lite is $1 per month, Acorns Personal is $3 per month, and Acorns Family is $5 each month.

Acorns offers a custodial brokerage account called Acorns Early for parents and grandparents who want to start an investment account for their family.

Acorns Early offers investing portfolios for kids with varying risk levels, so you can trust the account you're setting for your child. This app has the potential to teach minors about money management.

The nicest part about Acorns is that there is no minimum deposit required to get started, and you can make recurring contributions.

Acorns Early, a savings and investment account, is one of the greatest ways to start saving for your grandchild.

- Mighty oaks do grow from acorns. Develop your oak tree!

• Get investment accounts for you and your family, as well as retirement, checking, and opportunities to earn more money and expand your education, in less than 5 minutes.

• Known for automatically investing spare change through Round-Ups, this all-in-one financial app encourages younger generations to begin saving early.

•Only $1, $3, or $5 per month. (College students get in free.)

• Start with a $10 bonus.

CHAPTER THREE

OTHER ASSETS TO GIVE YOUR CHILDREN

There are savings bonds

In the 1990s, when my parents wanted to invest for their children, they bought savings bonds in their names. These were utilized by my parents to put money aside for me to pay for education.

Thankfully, I didn't need the money they had saved for me through savings bonds once I started college. I had worked hard enough to get scholarships and other financial aid to cover the costs of private education without having to go into my savings.

I was lucky in that I didn't require the college funds that my parents had set aside for me. Instead, as a teenager, I cashed these bonds and began investing in the stock market. I did well enough with my investments that I was able to use the earnings to purchase my first condo after graduation.

However, parents or grandparents who want to save money for their children or grandchildren can still do so directly through TreasuryDirect.gov.

You can still cash in your unused savings bonds at a bank, but you won't get tangible certificates.

Savings bonds are a good investment since they grow tax-free, but you must pay federal taxes on them when you redeem them.

Although interest rates on these bonds have dropped considerably in the recent decade, the Treasury promises that if you retain them for at least 20 years, you will at least double your original investment.

If you want to start saving at least 20 years in ahead and want a risk-free investment, look into savings bonds. Otherwise, you have more upside potential for providing assets for your children if you choose the investing strategies discussed above.

Money

The annual exclusion refers to a total of $15,000 in gifts that you may present to as many people as you choose each year.

Married couples can pool their yearly exclusions to contribute up to $30,000 ($15,000 x 2) to as many people as they like tax-free each year.

As a parent, you can give your child a monetary present up to the annual exclusion amount each year without paying taxes. These donations can be used to fund college, a car, a wedding, or even a down payment on a home.

If you give more than the yearly exclusion, the amount of your gifts is deducted from your lifetime exemption from inheritance taxes, which in 2021 will be $11.7 million for individuals and $23.4 million for couples.

How to Give Stock as a Gift

You have the option of donating shares without first selling them or directly gifting shares to your children. There are numerous possibilities available to you if you wish to invest in your children.

You may wish to boost their investing account balance by gifting stock now that you've examined some of the top money apps for teens and kids.

Transferring equities from your account to theirs entails additional stages and concerns that may not be apparent at first, as well as more steps than simply putting money.

- ***Taxes on Capital Gains***

When you sell your stocks and make a profit, you must pay capital gains taxes. When you transfer appreciating assets, such as shares, at a profit, neither side pays any capital gain at the time of transfer. The stock position transfers your basis and holding duration.

This could be a good method to teach your children about increasing their net worth.

- ***Gift Tax Regulations***

Next, as we've mentioned a few times now, you should be aware of gift tax restrictions. This won't be a problem for most people as long as the annual value of gifting stock is less than $15,000 per person (or $30,000 for married couples filing jointly).

- ***Financial Control***

Finally, think about how you'll keep these locations under your control. When you give stock as a gift, you relinquish control of the shares to the person who receives it.

Creating a trust is one option to invest for your children or grandchildren. The amounts available in this form of investment can be restricted.

CHAPTER FOUR

INVESTING FOR A CHILD'S FUTURE

Parents and grandparents must invest in their children's future achievement in order for them to be more successful than their parents.

Parents can demonstrate their commitment to seeing their children thrive rather than struggle by properly investing, even if it involves adjusting some aspects of their own lives.

You can provide your children the financial resources they need to live a better life by supporting them financially.

Many parents and grandparents hope that their children will one day be able to support themselves without the assistance of others. Investing in a child's future shows you are committed to this goal.

Best children Money Apps (Debit Cards, Investing & Mgmt)

Imagine how different the world would be if children were taught how to manage money from a young age.

Learning to live within your means, creating a budget that you stick to, getting started saving as a teenager or child, and planning for a safe retirement are just a few of the beneficial consequences that could occur.

Thankfully, this idealistic start to investing in your child's future isn't as far out of reach as it once was. In fact, there are a variety of materials available to assist you teach your children financial literacy.

You may even discover that your children are exposed to a fair bit of financial knowledge as a result of their daily interactions with media, such as video games, television, streaming services, and other forms of entertainment.

When it comes to teaching kids and teens about money management, this book will focus on the best money management applications for them.

Many of the applications are free and include some basic features, while others offer a free trial period to allow users to try out the app before committing to a monthly subscription.

Let's speak about a few related themes before we get into our selections for some of the finest apps for kids and their parents to manage money together on devices like iPhones, iPads, and Android smartphones.

Specifically, how children can learn about handling money in the real world and making their own spending decisions.

That means starting with banking and debit cards in today's cashless economy.

Making Your Own Spending Decisions

As a father of just one, it's been fascinating to watch my son let his mother and me make all of his decisions while he sat back and (largely) enjoyed the ride.

But, since learning to crawl, cruise, and now walk, he's learned to make his own decisions about what he wants to do and say.

Inevitably, this will force him to make more decisions. While we made these judgments for him, we want him to consider his options and make the best decision for himself.

Money will be one of the topics discussed. What to do with it, specifically.

My wife and I used to save our pocket money in piggy banks when we were kids. Our grocery shopping was done in person rather than online. Because debit cards and credit cards were not always the preferred means of payment, we would frequently observe our parents handling cash.

Money has become significantly less palpable as we spend more time online. As a result, how can we expect our children to learn about it and understand its significance? The several apps featured in this book provide the answer to this query.

You anticipate your son to pick up on money lessons from his mother, and you spend money at places like the grocery store, a restaurant, online, or anywhere else.

You want him to connect the cause and effect of these transactions, even if he won't see tangible money change hands in many of them. You want him to know how you and your partner handle money.

In particular, how you weigh your goals and needs and determine which is the most significant. You also want him to be able to recognize these things on his own and make his own decisions.

Once he has his right on these matters, you'll need to begin addressing how to make the purchases.

Understanding how credit cards function is becoming increasingly important. To begin, debit cards will suffice followed by credit cards as he becomes older. The finest debit cards for kids teach children how to budget and avoid overspending.

Because most youngsters won't be able to open a checking account on their own, you'll need to look into other debit card and banking choices for minors. Let's take a look at kids' debit cards.

Is It Possible To Get A Debit Card For My Child?
Your local bank is the ideal location to start thinking about getting a debit card for your child. Some institutions do not allow juveniles under the age of 16 to have debit cards in their own names, while others do so for children aged 13 and under.

However, simply putting a debit card in your child's hands might not be what you're looking for. You may desire more visibility and control over their spending in order to instill positive habits.

Having a joint prepaid debit card with a child, for example, allows you and your youngster to handle money together and agree on what the card can be used for.

These cards provide kids the control they seek over their money while enabling parents to monitor their spending and offer assistance as needed. Let's take a look at some of the best prepaid debit card programs for kids and how to enroll.

When looking for debit cards and banking solutions for your children, keep in mind the features that come standard with the bank account and debit cards.

Parents should seek for features such as no or minimal fees for funding and maintaining the jointly-managed account, conveniently accessible and adjustable online account monitoring, simple (ideally free) ATM access, and the opportunity to set spending limitations within agreed-upon parameters.

In this section of the book about the best debit cards for kids, I've analyzed all of the important considerations you should make.

I've reviewed a few apps that let you use some or all of these functions in the sections below.

Greenlight Card (Investment Account with Debit Card).

Greenlight allows parents to restrict where their children can spend money by limiting the establishments that accept their cards. Parents can receive notifications when money is spent on the Greenlight debit card, as well as the amount spent.

Parents can also open a custodial brokerage account for their children to begin investing in stocks and index funds.

Greenlight functions similarly to a prepaid debit card, allowing you to load money onto the card for your child to use at approved locations to pay for charges.

You can load as much money as you want onto the card, and your child will be able to make allowed purchases as long as the card has a money balance.

Greenlight costs $4.99 a month for a family of up to five children. Replacement cards are $3.50 apiece, but the first month is free. You can obtain rapid shipping for $24.99 if you need to replace your card right away.

This company also offers a customised card with your own photo or design for $9.99 every year. Greenlight does not give interest, but you and your child can set up "parent-paid interest" where you pay the bill and pay interest on accounts for up to five children.

If your child requests additional funds, you can have them snap a photo of the purchase they wish to make and submit it to you for approval. This offers you control and allows your children to talk about why a particular purchase is a good or terrible choice.

If your child works, he or she can put money on the card as well.

The Greenlight debit card is a good option for parents who want to instill in their children the value of saving money and making wise financial decisions.

This financial product can be a useful teaching tool for youngsters to understand why saving is important, as well as for parents to make giving an allowance or keeping track of chores easier.

It's also a rapidly developing app that many parents are turning to in order to raise financially savvy children.

Among all the cards we looked at, the Greenlight Mastercard Debit Card has the best combination of features, including a simple mobile app. Who says youngsters can't have a debit card of their own? Greenlight is our #1 choice among the many options available to parents today.

- Greenlight provides configurable parental restrictions for each child as well as real-time transaction notifications.

- Parents can use this app to teach their children how to invest with a custodial account through Greenlight Max, which is the only debit card that allows you to choose the specific stores where they can use the card.

goHenry

goHenry is a financial app for teenagers that includes a debit card. You have a personal online account that is linked to each of your children's accounts.

The company's app and online account site allow you to control all of the money in each account.

Each child will have their own goHenry debit card, which will include parental controls that you may establish for them.

The option to spend only the money available on the card is a good feature of goHenry, since it eliminates the need to worry about costly overdraft fees or debt accumulation.

You create a goHenry account, get your children's debit cards in the mail in 7-8 business days, set up an automated weekly allowance transfer into their accounts, and establish one-time or weekly spending limits.

This will keep your children's spending under control, and you'll be able to ban and unblock the card as needed, as well as determine which retailers they can buy at.

With time, the restrictions provided by the app and the advice you provide can assist your children in developing healthy money habits as they earn, save, spend, and contribute.

For customer service, goHenry is one of the finest debit cards for kids.

They provide phone support 24 hours a day, email support, and social media participation to ensure that users can address their problems swiftly and easily.

• A financial app and debit card aimed at providing a secure financial future for young people aged 6 to 18.

• With goHenry, kids may earn allowance, complete chores, create savings goals, donate to charity, and bank.

• Use the app to improve your financial literacy.

- Cost: Free for the first month, then $3.99 per child per month.

FamZoo

Another prepaid debit card service that parents can use to keep track on their children's spending is FamZoo. It works by allowing parents to deposit funds into their child's account and then allowing the card to operate with a pre-loaded balance. The cards can be loaded with money at any time.

FamZoo functions similarly to a traditional checking account with a linked debit card, with the exception that FamZoo ensures that the account is not subject to overdraft fees, saving you money.

Adults are able to keep track of the transactions that are taking place. This investing on app costs $5.99 per month after a free trial, but the price drops if you pay in advance.

- FamZoo is a prepaid debit card that allows families to teach their children good financial habits from a young age.

- It comes with a financial app that allows you to keep track of your transactions.

- Price: Free trial, then $5.99 per month after that.

Rated 4.6 on the App Store.

Acorns

Acorns has grown to be one of the most popular investment apps for minors and young adults, but it also provides a comprehensive money management platform that goes beyond investing. The whole array of services includes the ability to open custodial accounts for kids to invest in, as well as ordinary and retirement investment accounts for adults and a bank account with a linked debit card.

When you sign up for the Acorns Spend program, you'll have a bank account with up to $250k in FDIC insurance protection.

It also employs Acorns' "Round Ups" feature, which rounds up purchases to the nearest dollar and invests the difference between the transaction amount and the entire dollar.

Using this tool, the firm claims to assist users invest an average of $30 every month.

Although Acorns is not a free stock trading program, it does offer the following subscription options:

- Acorns Lite ($1/month): This plan includes the Acorns Invest plan, which invests spare change via the famous "Round-Ups" feature, awards bonus investments, and gives you access to financial literacy articles.

- Acorns Personal ($3/month): Includes everything in Acorns Lite (Investing), plus Acorns Later for tax-advantaged investing alternatives like IRAs and Acorns Spend. This service functions as a bank account, with free withdrawals at over 55,000 ATMs around the country, no account fees, and the opportunity to earn up to 10% bonus investments.

- Acorns Family ($5/month): Includes Acorns Invest, Later, and Spend, as well as Acorns Early. As a minor, you can open a custodial account for your child and start investing in it.

For a limited time, the service is also offering a $10 sign-up incentive to new users. This can be beneficial in learning how to begin investing.

- Mighty oaks do grow from acorns. Develop your oak tree!

- Get investment accounts for you and your family, as well as retirement, checking, and opportunities to earn more money and expand your education, in under 5 minutes.

• Known for automatically investing spare change through Round-Ups, this all-in-one financial app encourages younger generations to begin saving early.

• Only $1, $3, or $5 every month. College students get in free.

• You get a $10 bonus just for signing up.

Stash

• Price: $1/month for beginners, $3/month for growth, and $9/month for Stash+.

Stash, a major all-in-one financial platform that offers a mobile-friendly banking account, is another software that has made our list twice. With no hidden costs, no minimum deposit or balance requirements, and no ATM fees, Stash could be a good option for people who want to do their banking and investing on the same platform.

When you use your Stock-Back card to make qualified purchases at stores like Walmart, Amazon, and others, you'll earn Stock-Back Rewards.

If you're a young adult, you might wish to utilize Stash to invest money through monthly automated transfers or by "rounding up" purchases made on a linked debit card so that the leftover change goes to your personal portfolio.

Financial education resources are also available through Stash to help you improve your financial literacy. It covers a wide range of topics, including investment, money management, and financial planning.

The following are the specifics of the Stash bank account:

• Minimum Deposit and Balance Requirements: There is no minimum daily balance requirement, however to utilize your Stash Online Banking account, you must first open a Stash Invest account.

• No yield, but every qualified transaction made with the Stock-Back card earns you Stock-Back rewards.

• Incentives and Rewards: Every qualified debit card purchase earns you Stock-Back rewards. Earn 0.125 percent Stock-Back points on regular transactions and up to 5% Stock-Back rewards on purchases with qualified merchants9. When you direct deposit your income into your Stash banking account, you can get paid up to two days early and have access to thousands of fee-free ATMs7.

• Fees for using out-of-network ATMs2 are a possibility.

With the help of the personal finance software Stash, normal people may now invest easily and affordably.

• Stash will give you a $5 sign up bonus if you sign up and make a $5 deposit.

• Cost: $1/month for beginners, $3/month for growth, and $9/month for Stash+.

CHAPTER FIVE

OTHER EXCELLENT INVESTMENT APPS FOR CHILDREN

First and foremost, children must comprehend the worth of money and how it may be used to save for significant purchases or spent on daily necessities. Kids will need to manage and invest their money in order to get the most out of it.

When done correctly, this will assist children in developing financial literacy skills, reducing their anxiety of financial matters, and putting them on a healthier financial path. Some of the top investing and money management applications for kids and teenagers are listed below.

Both applications require a parent or guardian to open if the account owner is a minor, however after the account owner reaches the age of majority, the account will be transferred to the account owner's name (18 or 21 in some states for financial items).

Acorns (bonus of $10)

Holy Doubletake, Batman! Is that app making this list again? You're right.

Acorns make an appearance on this list of the top money apps for kids for the second time. Because it also serves as an all-in-one financial health app, it appears in the kids investing app section this time.

When your child reaches the age of majority in your state, you can open a custodial account in his or her name. You can pool your resources and make contributions to achieve your financial goals over time.

Consider signing up for this platform so that your children can learn how to handle money and invest.

• Mighty oaks do grow from acorns. Develop your oak tree!

• Get investment accounts for you and your family, as well as retirement, checking, and opportunities to earn more money and expand your education, in under 5 minutes.

• Known for automatically investing spare change through Round-Ups, this all-in-one financial app encourages younger generations to begin saving early.

• Only $1, $3, or $5 every month. (College students get in free.)

• Start with a $10 bonus.

Greenlight

• Price: Free one-month trial, then $7.98 per month for the Greenlight Card + Invest package.

Is there a new app on this list of the top money apps for kids? You are correct.

Greenlight + Invest is a kids' investing account that includes a debit card and a bank account.

It's simple to use and can be used as both a savings account and a banking app for teenagers. The app will cover the fundamentals of investing, such as how to invest in stocks and ETFs.

Because it necessitates connected accounts from the custodians' banks or brokerages, it works best if parents and/or grandparents are involved in the process.

In addition, trades in the investment account must be approved by parents and guardians.

With real money, real stocks, and real-life courses, the all-in-one package teaches them critical financial skills including money management and investment concepts.

• Purchase fractional shares of firms your children admire using the investing function (kid-friendly stocks).

- No trading commissions beyond the monthly subscription price.

- You can actually invest with fractional shares with as little as $1 in your account.

- Every trade on individual stocks and ETFs with a market value of $1 billion or more must be approved by parents directly in the app.

Consider opening a Greenlight Card + Invest account for your children today to begin investing in a custodial brokerage account. The first month is completely free to test the product and determine whether it satisfies your demands for making one of the best investments for children.

- Greenlight provides configurable parental restrictions for each child as well as real-time transaction notifications.

- Parents can use this app to teach their children how to invest with a custodial account through Greenlight Max, which is the only debit card that allows you to choose the specific stores where they can use the card.

EarlyBird ($10 Bonus)

• Cost: $1 each month (free for the first $200 managed); $2 per gift (for the giver).

EarlyBird is a mobile app that allows parents and guardians to set up a UGMA account for their children to receive money for investments.

This software makes it simple and affordable to give money to a child, with funds available for any expenses that benefit the youngster.

When giving a gift, givers can film a video to accompany it, personalizing these once-in-a-lifetime occasions. You can text a link from the app to the recipient's phone number if you want to gift but they don't have an account.

You can choose from five alternative portfolios when opening an account to invest for your children, ranging from prudent (100 percent bond ETFs) to adventurous (100 percent stock ETFs).

To meet your investing goals, all portfolios rely on diverse ETFs, which eliminate the complexity of completing your own research or selecting specific stocks.

You can open an account for free and manage the first $200, after which the account will charge $1 per month per child. In addition, the giver must pay a $2 processing fee for each gift made.

Consider signing up for an EarlyBird account today and receiving $10 to get you started.

• Through custodial accounts, EarlyBird allows parents, relatives, and friends to invest in the next generation.

• Make financial investments in children by sending and receiving money gifts.

• Provides fixed ETF-based investment portfolios based on a child's age, investment goals, time horizon, risk tolerance, and other criteria.

Stash ($5 Bonus)
• Monthly subscriptions start at $1.

Wait; is that Stash all over again? That's correct. As an all-in-one personal finance management platform, Stash makes another appearance on our list.

Stash, as previously indicated, features mobile-friendly investment software as well as a bank account and debit card.

Create an account today to start investing and managing your money using this amazing one-stop shop solution.

They even provide a no-risk sign-up bonus to get you started.

• Stash is a personal finance app that makes investing simple and accessible to regular Americans. Stash will give you a $5 sign up bonus if you sign up and make a $5 deposit.

M1 Finance (bonus of $30)

Your financial needs can be met in one place with M1 Finance.You may use the app to invest, borrow, and spend money, as well as open an M1 Finance custodial account or a custodial Roth IRA for your children.

However, in order to use the service, you must first join up for M1 Plus. Keep an eye out for when the firm runs an offer where you can sample it for free.

Money held in the app's free checking account is insured by the Federal Deposit Insurance Corporation (FDIC) and is part of the secure M1 Finance financial app experience.

• M1 Finance's Smart Money Management allows you the freedom and flexibility to invest, borrow, and spend your money automatically, with high-yield checking and cheap borrowing rates accessible.

• Price: M1 Plus is $125 per year and includes free trades.

UNest ($25 Bonus)

• Cost: $3 per month for regular, $6 per month for family

You can use UNest to gain flexibility in saving for all of your children's critical life phases, like as college, a first car, or a home.

Because it allows parents to invest in their children's names through a custodial account, this platform serves as an excellent investment app for children.

Through the UNest partner program, UNest account holders can obtain bonuses for their children's UNest accounts from companies such as Disney, AT&T, Uber, DoorDash, Levis, and others.

For a limited time, new users of the app can get a $25 credit when they open and fund an account with at least $25.

UNest is a tax-advantaged savings account for children. It enables children to save for a college education, a first car, a house, a wedding, or even their adult financial security.

• Investment possibilities - 5 options to choose from depending on your needs.

• Taxes - annual tax benefits of $2,200 and the first $1,100 in earnings are tax-free.

CHAPTER SIX

CHILDREN'S ALLOWANCE APPS

Developing a relationship between labor and money at a young age is a desirable habit to acquire. This can encourage children to work hard and develop personal savings goals.

They can also be rewarded for their patience by achieving a goal of making a purchase they really want.

The top allowance and chore apps for kids below help parents and children manage allowance payments and achieve critical financial goals.

Rooster Money

- Price: Rooster Money Virtual Tracker is free, while Rooster Plus is $18.99 per year with a 30-day free trial.

Rooster Money is an app that helps parents to keep track of all of their children's allowances in one place, as well as provide enjoyable activities for them to engage in while learning about money.

The software assists parents in guiding their children through crucial financial milestones by using a star chart to teach as a rewards system in their early years, and eventually introducing a payment card as they get older.

The software wants money to be a part of the conversation, and it wants to assist you in doing so with your kids. Dispelling this stigma at a young age can help children develop financial confidence.

• Rooster Money aims to break the stigma of discussing money by establishing a clear rewards system for reaching certain financial milestones. As your children get older and wish to manage their own money, the program offers a free virtual tracker and can also include a debit card.

Savings Spree

• Price: $5.99; only available for iOS.

The principle of tiny purchases adding up in the long term is emphasized in this gamified app. It also shows the reverse effect by demonstrating how tiny, consistent saves can add up to a large sum over time.

The software functions in the same way as a game show hosted by a talking pig. Users can take on the role of participants on the game show to discover how everyday lifestyle adjustments can affect your long-term financial potential.

It also depicts the impact of unforeseen expenses that may arise and ruin your financial objectives. The proposed approach is to have a well funded emergency fund.

While the concepts presented in this program are more appropriate for younger teens than older teens and young adults, they are important to grasp at any age.

PiggyBot.
• Price: Free; only available on iOS

This program functions as an allowance app, allowing children to spend, share, and save money wisely. PiggyBot lets users to keep track of allowance spending and savings, as well as IOUs and late allowance payments.

This program doesn't use currency; instead, it keeps track of a virtual balance you have on hand. Consider it a virtual IOU monitoring app, with individual Spend-It, Share-It, and Save-It accounts for each child.

You can work together to develop shared goals for meeting your desires and needs, as well as learning how to distinguish between them. When you're ready to transfer to spending money in pre-approved stores, this app would work well with Greenlight's debit card and bank account.

iAllowance.

• Price: $2.99; only available for iOS.

iAllowance claims to have done over 30 million chores and handed out over 20 million allowances through the app. You can manage your children's finances and teach them about saving and spending money by using virtual piggy banks.

You can use a service like Stash, Greenlight, or Acorns to set up weekly allowance payments that are automatically transferred to your teen's bank account at regular intervals.

It's a win-win situation because you won't have to repeatedly withdraw cash and your child will always receive their money on time. If your adolescent is in charge of tasks, you can use iAllowance to keep track of them and even send push notifications for those that have yet to be completed.

CHAPTER SEVEN

EVERYTHING YOU NEED TO KNOW ABOUT DEBIT CARDS AND CHILDREN

Money apps can help children quickly learn financial skills by gamifying the themes and include adults in the discourse. Better guidance and life outcomes may result as a result of this.

Thankfully, teaching children about money does not have to be a tedious task.

Teaching youngsters how to spend and save wisely can be challenging, but it doesn't have to be. A debit card can be a useful instructional tool, especially if the youngster is in responsible of their own spending and has parental guardrails in place.

Debit cards are the first step toward financial responsibility since they allow children to take control of their spending and offer them a taste of how to manage money on their own.

This portion of the book will go through some of the best debit cards for kids and teens so you can pick one that will suit your child's needs the best!

What Is A Children's Debit Card?

Children must wait until they attain the age of majority in their state, which is usually 18 years old, before they can open their own bank account. One option for parents is to open a subaccount from their personal bank account and provide their children with a card to use.

Before acquiring a card, your youngster will most likely need to be at least 13 years old.

These accounts, on the other hand, may not include the specific spending limitations, parental oversight, or feature-rich mobile apps that many new debit cards for kids do. Some new apps even allow you to freeze the card or set spending limits for your youngster.

Because you can set parental controls on these cards, they can also be used as a prepaid debit card. Traditional banks or prepaid debit cards may not allow you to do this beyond maintaining a specific account balance.

Is It Possible To Get A Debit Card For A Child Under The Age Of 13?

In most cases, you consider your existing circumstances and begin weighing possibilities based on what you know. As a result, your own bank is the most likely place to start thinking about getting a debit card for your child.

Though laws differ by financial institution, some do not allow kids under the age of 16 to have debit cards in their own names. Others opt to give them to children aged 13 and under.

You don't want to merely hand your youngster a debit card, even if you can get one from your current bank. You may desire more visibility and control over their spending in order to instill positive habits.

A joint prepaid debit card with your child, for example, allows you and your youngster to handle money together and agree on what the card can be used for.

These cards provide kids the control they seek over their money while enabling parents to monitor their spending and offer assistance as needed.

Traditional banks don't always have these controls available, making account administration a challenging task without the proper tools.

Instead, a new generation of financial companies has evolved to empower parents to make financial decisions with their children and to provide them with the tools they need to handle money in the way they choose.

Let's have a look at some of the best debit cards for children and teenagers now. Then we'll go through the benefits of the best prepaid debit card programs for kids and how to enroll.

Which Debit Cards Are Best For Kids And Teens?

Below you'll find a selection of the finest debit cards for kids and teens that should suit your needs. Choose the one that makes the most sense for your needs after carefully examining each.

Best Rated Overall
Greenlight

Greenlight allows parents to restrict where their children can spend money by limiting the establishments that accept their cards. Parents can receive notifications about when and how much money is spent on their children's Greenlight debit card.

Parents can also open an investment account for their children to get them started investing in stocks and index funds.

Greenlight functions similarly to a prepaid debit card, allowing you to load money onto the card for your child to use at approved locations to pay for charges.

You can load as much money as you want onto the card, and your child will be able to make allowed purchases as long as the card has a money balance.

Greenlight costs $4.99 a month for a family of up to five children. Replacement cards cost $3.50 apiece, but the first time you get one is free. You can obtain rapid shipping for $24.99 if you need to replace your card right away.

For $9.99 every year, you can get a personalized card with your own photo or design.

Greenlight is the only prepaid debit card for kids and teens that offers interest, and you can set up "parent-paid interest" between you and your child. This permits you to foot the bill and pay interest on up to five children's accounts.

If your child requests additional funds, you can have them snap a photo of the purchase they wish to make and submit it to you for approval. This offers you control and allows your children to discuss why a purchase is a good or terrible idea with you.

If your child has a job, he or she can also contribute money to the card through direct deposit.

The Greenlight debit card is a good option for parents who want to instill in their children the value of saving money and making wise financial decisions.

This financial product can be a useful teaching tool for youngsters to understand why saving is important, as well as for parents to make giving an allowance or keeping track of chores easier.

It's also a rapidly developing app that many parents are turning to in order to raise financially savvy children. The product has no minimum age requirement, but it is recommended that you begin at the age of six or later.

Among all the cards we tested, the Greenlight Mastercard Debit Card for Kids had the best combination of features, including a simple mobile app.

Who says youngsters can't have a debit card of their own? Greenlight is our #1 choice among the many options available to parents today.

• Greenlight provides configurable parental restrictions for each child as well as real-time transaction notifications.

- Greenlight is the only debit card that allows you to specify which stores your children can use the card at, and parents can use Greenlight Max to educate their children how to invest with a custodial account.

The Best Free Debit Card For Children And Adolescents
Chase First Banking

Are you ready to teach your children about money but aren't sure if you have the time, patience, or competence to do so?

Chase First Banking provides uncomplicated banking for both of you in one convenient location: the Chase Mobile App, which is available for download for free. With this mobile app, you can manage all of your accounts and avoid fees, as well as withdraw money from 16,000 Chase ATMs across the country.

One of the greatest free debit cards for kids and teens that works anywhere Visa is accepted is at the heart of Chase First Banking.

Do you want to know how much your child spends and saves? In your Chase Mobile app, you may establish spending alerts and limits, as well as specified areas.

Using the Chase Mobile app, teach your kids how to spend, save, and earn. Chase First Banking makes it easier for parents to teach their children about money by providing them the control they want while also giving them the freedom they need to learn.

To get started, you must first be a Chase customer with a Chase checking account that qualifies.

• With Chase Total Checking, you'll have access to 16,000 Chase ATMs and over 4,700 branches, as well as a $225 sign-up bonus if you set up direct deposit within 90 days of enrolling in the coupon. If you meet specific requirements, you can pay no monthly costs.

• Chase Secure Banking includes the same Chase ATMs and branch locations as Chase Regular Banking, as well as a $100 sign-up incentive if you complete certain qualifying activities and meet specific criteria.

You can apply for a Chase First Banking account for your child once you have opened a qualified Chase Checking account.

• Chase First Banking provides easy banking for both of you in one place: the Chase Mobile App, which is available for free.

- In your Chase Mobile app, you may establish spending alerts and limits, as well as specified areas.

- With Chase First Banking, you can teach your kids how to spend, save, and earn. The account assists parents in teaching their children about money by giving them the control they desire while allowing children the freedom they require to learn.

The Best For Customer Service
. **goHenry**

Parents may monitor and manage their children's account balances with goHenry, a banking software for minors that comes with prepaid debit cards. You have a personal online account that is linked to each of your children's accounts.

The company's app and online account site allow you to control all of the money in each account.

Each child will have their own goHenry debit card, which will include parental controls that you may establish for them.

The option to spend only the money available on the card is a good feature of goHenry, since it eliminates the need to worry about costly overdraft fees or debt accumulation.

You create a goHenry account, get your children's debit cards in the mail in 7-8 business days, set up an automated weekly allowance transfer into their accounts, and establish one-time or weekly spending limits.

This will keep your children's spending under control, and you'll be able to ban and unblock the card as needed, as well as determine which retailers they can buy at.

With time, the restrictions provided by the app and the advice you provide can assist your children in developing healthy money habits as they earn, save, spend, and contribute.

For customer service, goHenry is one of the finest debit cards for kids. They provide phone support 24 hours a day, email support, and social media participation to ensure that users can address their problems swiftly and easily.

The product has no minimum age requirement, but it is recommended that you begin at the age of six or later.

- Kids can earn allowance, do chores, establish savings goals, give to charity, and bank with goHenry, a financial app and debit card designed to give young people aged 6 to 18 a bright financial future.

- Cost: Free for the first month, then $3.99 per child per month

- Use the app to develop a strong financial foundation.

The Best For Value
BusyKid

- Cost: $19.99 per year for the first card, $7.99 per year for each additional card.

Are you seeking for a way to teach your children about money by having them do chores, earn an allowance, and manage their money using prepaid debit cards for children?

BusyKid is a parent-approved, award-winning software that teaches youngsters about money. It's a good approach to teach your kids how to handle their money and to teach them vital financial concepts.

With just one swipe of the BusyKid Visa Prepaid Spend Card, they may spend their money in stores or online. You can even automate your savings. The product has no minimum age restriction, but it is suggested that you begin sooner rather than later.

Your child will be able to earn real money while learning key financial skills like as budgeting, saving, and giving back by completing chores and responsibilities around the house each week.

Plus, they'll have a blast participating in BusyKid's weekly challenges and earning prizes from businesses like Disney!

BusyKid is a fun, interactive kid chore app with a debit card that will help kids learn and practice vital life lessons right in their hands.

They can make money, save money, invest money, contribute money, and spend money all while having fun! And it couldn't be much easier.

BusyKid is a parent-approved, award-winning app that teaches youngsters about money. It has four main features:

Each Friday, parents assign chores, and the allowance is instantly paid!

• Earn - Children can earn money by performing activities set by their parents.

- Save - They can automatically save up to 10% of their weekly stipend.

- Donate - They can help others by donating 1% of their earnings to charity.

- Spend — When they're ready, BusyKid offers a Visa Prepaid Spend Card, ensuring that youngsters never go without cash.

If your children are to get paid on Friday, parents must authorize the Payday text message delivered through the app each Thursday.

BusyKid's reloadable Visa Prepaid Spend debit cards are issued by Visa, and there is a $7.99 annual cost per card after the first one that comes with the account. Different fees apply to a variety of other actions you can perform using the app and the card.

Finally, BusyKid allows children to use the program to invest their profits. To do so, you'll need to create a separate Stockpile custodial account.

Axos Bank First Checking Debit Card for Teens
Axos Bank has the best free debit card for teenagers. Axos Bank's First Checking is the best beginner checking account for teenagers, complete with a debit card. The

world of banking can be intimidating, but not with Axos' First Checking Account's simplicity and power.

The account functions as a joint account between a parent or guardian and their teen, with simple, adjustable parental controls and a debit card dashboard.

A handy smartphone app or an online desktop interface allows parents and kids to oversee practically every aspect of the banking experience. Ideal for modern families who are constantly on the move.

Axos Bank's First Checking account gives kids their first taste of financial independence by providing them with their own checking account (which earns interest!) and a free debit card with daily cash withdrawal and purchase limitations of $100 and $500, respectively.

This prevents teenagers from getting too carried away with the money in their account.

You can also receive up to $12 in domestic ATM charge reimbursements per month, as well as avoid any monthly maintenance, overdraft, or non-sufficient funds penalties, thereby making the account free!

Biometric authentication mechanisms such as fingerprint readers, voiceprints, and face recognition provide the account with the highest level of protection.

The product has a 13-year-old minimum age requirement, and after you reach the age of majority, it will convert to an Axos Checking Account.

• For youths aged 13 to 17, a joint checking account is available.

• There are no monthly fees for overdrafts or insufficient cash.

• Account alerts on a debit card.

• Receive a dividend of up to 0.10 percent annually.

• Reimbursement of up to $12 in domestic ATM fees each month.

• Limits on daily transactions ($100 cash, $500 debit).

Famzoo Is The Best For Financial Education
• Price: Free trial, then $5.99 per family every month]

FamZoo is another solution for parents who want to regulate their children's spending by opening prepaid debit cards.

It works by allowing parents to deposit funds into their child's account and then allowing the card to operate with a pre-loaded balance. The cards can be loaded with money at any time.

FamZoo functions similarly to a traditional checking account with a linked debit card, with the exception that FamZoo ensures that the account is not subject to overdraft fees, saving you money.

Adults are able to keep track of the transactions that are taking place. This app costs $5.99 per month after a free trial, but the price drops if you pay in advance.

FamZoo is our best educational option because to its extensive financial education library, which adds to its total value.

The product has no minimum age restriction, but it is suggested that you begin sooner rather than later.

- FamZoo is a prepaid debit card that allows families to teach their children good financial habits from a young age.

- It comes with a financial app that allows you to keep track of your transactions.

Acorns are the best for long-term growth

Acorns has grown to be one of the most popular financial apps for minors and young adults, but it also provides a comprehensive money management platform that goes beyond investment.

The whole array of services includes the ability to open custodial accounts for kids to invest in, as well as ordinary and retirement investment accounts for adults and a bank account with a linked debit card.

When you sign up for the Acorns Spend product (offered under the Acorns Personal and Acorns Family plans), you'll get a bank account with up to $250k in FDIC insurance.

It also employs Acorns' "Round Ups" feature, which rounds up purchases to the nearest dollar and invests the difference between the transaction amount and the entire dollar. Using this tool, the firm claims to assist users invest an average of $30 every month.

Although Acorns is not a free stock trading program, it does offer the following subscription options:

- Acorns Lite ($1/mo): This plan includes the Acorns Invest plan, which invests spare change via the famous

"Round-Ups" feature, awards extra investments, and gives you access to financial literacy articles.

• Acorns Personal ($3/mo): Includes everything in Acorns Lite (Investing), plus Acorns Later for tax-advantaged investing options including individual retirement accounts (IRAs) and Acorns Spend for youngsters and teens with linked debit cards. This service functions as a bank account, with free withdrawals at over 55,000 ATMs around the country, no account or purchase fees, and the opportunity to earn up to 10% bonus investments.

• Acorns Family ($5/month): Includes Acorns Invest, Later, and Spend, as well as Acorns Early. As a minor, you can open a custodial account for your child and start investing in it.

For a limited time, the service is also offering a $10 sign-up incentive to new users.

• Mighty oaks do grow from acorns. Develop your oak tree!

(Acorns grow into gigantic oaks, implying that anything big and successful started small and insignificantly.) Naturally, Henry Ford did not begin his business by opening hundreds of plants in his first year.

- Get investment accounts for you and your family, as well as retirement, checking, and opportunities to earn more money and expand your education, in less than 5 minutes.

- Known for automatically investing spare change through Round-Ups, this all-in-one financial app encourages younger generations to begin saving early.

Current: The Best For Product Features And Innovation.

- Cost: $36 per teen per year.

Current is a banking app for families of all sizes. You may use the Current app to keep track of your teen's spending in real time, establish spending limitations, and even block specific merchants on Visa-enabled prepaid debit cards.

You also have the peace of mind that comes with knowing that their money is secure because it isn't in cash. Furthermore, there are no fees or interest charges for student accounts, so there are no unpleasant surprises when bills arrive.

Current assists parents in instilling financial responsibility in their children while also providing a means for them to learn without the temptations that come with having cash around the house.

This implies that both parents and children will have less to worry about! With Current, your adolescent will be able to do everything from paying back pals to purchasing groceries at the store—all while remaining safe and secure.

Teens will also be able to learn financial responsibility and budgeting at a young age. They will be able to expand their savings and become closer to financial independence as a result of this.

Although there is no declared minimum age requirement for the product, the marketing suggests that the intended demographic is a Teen Account. As a result, you may be able to register an account for your child before they reach this age.

• Real-time money transfers and spending alerts

• Encourages adolescent financial responsibility.

• Families can control their money together, saving for goals and working toward financial goals, thanks to the ability of parents to set spending restrictions and block specific merchants.

Stash Is The Best Option When Approaching Finances For The First Time.

• Cost: $1/month for beginners, $3/month for growth, and $9/month for Stash+1.

Stash is a popular all-in-one financial platform that includes a mobile banking account. With no hidden banking fees, no minimum deposit or balance requirements, and no ATM fees, Stash could be a good option for people who want to do their banking and investing in one place.

When you use your Stock-Back card to make qualified purchases at stores like Walmart, Amazon, and others, you'll earn Stock-Back Rewards.

If you're a young adult, you might wish to utilize Stash to invest money through monthly automated transfers or by "rounding up" purchases made on a linked debit card so that the leftover change goes to your personal portfolio.

Financial education resources are also available through Stash to help you improve your financial literacy. It covers a wide range of topics, including investment, money management, and financial planning.

The following are the specifics of the Stash bank account:

• Minimum Deposit and Balance Requirements: There is no minimum daily balance requirement, however to utilize your Stash Online Banking account, you must first open a Stash Invest account.

• No yield, but every qualified transaction made with the Stock-Back card earns you Stock-Back rewards.

• Incentives and Rewards: Every qualified debit card purchase earns you Stock-Back rewards. Earn 0.125 percent Stock-Back rewards on everyday transactions and up to 5% Stock-Back rewards on purchases with qualified merchants. When you direct deposit your money into your Stash banking account, you can get paid up to two days early and have access to thousands of fee-free ATMs.

• Fees for using out-of-network ATMs are a possibility.

• Stash is a personal finance app that makes investing simple and accessible to regular Americans.

• Stash will give you a $5 sign up bonus if you sign up and make a $5 deposit.

Roostermoney: The Best App For Handling Allowances.

• Price: Virtual Tracker is free, while Rooster Plus is $18.99 per year with a 30-day free trial.

Rooster Money is an app that helps parents to keep track of all of their children's allowances in one place, as well as provide enjoyable activities for them to engage in while learning about money.

The software assists parents in guiding their children through crucial financial milestones by teaching them how to use a star chart as a rewards system in their younger years and introducing a credit or debit card as they get older.

The software wants money to be a part of the conversation, and it wants to assist you in doing so with your kids. Dispelling this stigma at a young age can help children develop financial confidence.

• Rooster Money aims to break the stigma of discussing money by establishing a clear rewards system for reaching certain financial milestones.

• As your children get older and wish to manage their own money, the program offers a free virtual tracker and can also include a debit card.

M1 Finance Is The Best For Financial Automation.
For all of your financial needs, M1 Finance is the place to go. You can invest, borrow, and spend with the app, but you can also open an M1 Finance custodial account to allow your children to use it as an investment app.

This is one of the greatest custodian accounts because they allow custodial IRAs. However, in order to use the service, you must first join up for M1 Plus. Keep an eye out for when the firm runs an offer where you can sample it for free.

When it comes to money management and associated debit cards, money held in the app's free checking account is insured by the Federal Deposit Insurance Corporation (FDIC) and is part of the secure M1 Finance financial app experience.

• M1 Finance's Smart Money Management allows you the freedom and flexibility to invest, borrow, and spend your money automatically, with high-yield checking and cheap borrowing rates accessible.

Jassby Virtual Debit Card For Kids.
• Price: Free, although inactivity after 6 months may result in monthly costs. Jassby is a free mobile wallet

program that allows families to keep track of chores, allowance payments, and debit card spending.

Parents and guardians can use the app to split money with their children while also teaching them important financial literacy skills. The service is currently only available as an iOS app.

The Jassby Virtual Debit Card allows kids to spend their allowance at the Jassby Shop or anywhere else that accepts Apple Pay.

Gift cards to stores and companies that youngsters are likely to want to spend their allowance on are available in the shop. Apple's App Store and iTunes, Nintendo's PlayStation Store, Microsoft's Rewards program, and other locations are examples.

Clothing stores, electronics stores, restaurants, entertainment, and more can all be found here. You can alternatively contribute the allowance money to one of the Jassby Shop's qualified charities.

If at least one family Jassby Virtual Debit Card makes a purchase each month, there are no monthly fees for accounts that use purchases on the fully contactless debit card for youngsters.

If there is no activity for the first six months after the account is opened, Jassby will charge a $2.99 monthly fee for each calendar month.

Finally, Jassby provides online e-learning resources for children to learn about personal finance and other enjoyable activities. You can, for example, buy a CodeWizardsHQ online coding education package for youngsters and teens aged 8 to 18.

All e-learning programs at the Jassby Shop, according to Jassby, are family-friendly and may be paid for with an allowance earned and saved using the Jassby app.

Honorable Mention: Nationwide Bank First Checking Offers A Free Teen Debit Card.

With an adolescent checking account product that is nearly identical to Axos' First Checking, Nationwide's First Checking serves as the ultimate beginner checking account with debit card for teenagers. Because of their features and low price, we believe they both deserve to be on our list.

This Nationwide account, like Axos' First Checking, functions as a joint account between a parent or guardian and their kid, with easy-to-set, configurable parental controls and a debit card dashboard.

With the same features and functionality, the only difference is that you can start collecting interest with a $0 amount in your account.

This equates to 0.1 percent APY as of summer 2021, which is a competitive rate for a simple teen checking account and debit card combination.

- For youths aged 13 to 17, a joint checking account is available.

- There are no monthly fees for overdrafts or insufficient cash.

- Account alerts on a debit card.

- Earn up to 0.10 percent annual percentage yield (APY) on a $0 account balance.

- Reimbursement of up to $12 in domestic ATM fees each month.

- Limits on daily transactions ($100 cash, $500 debit).

What Should a Debit Card for Children Include?

It can be difficult to select the best debit cards for children. They're no longer children, and as teenagers and eventually adults, they'll need to learn how to manage their finances.

Monthly fees, ATM withdrawal restrictions, direct deposit availability, rapid money transfer, access to the child's account for establishing spending limitations, overdraft penalties, incentive programs, and other aspects should all be considered when selecting a debit card for children.

CHAPTER EIGHT

FEATURES TO LOOK FOR IN KIDS AND TEENS DEBIT CARDS

Below, let me walk you through all of the features you should look for in the debit cards kids and teens can use.

1. Making A Direct Deposit

Direct deposit is one of the nicest features that may be accessible on debit cards for kids. Instead of receiving an envelope from work and passing it over to mum or dad for money management, a child's wage will be deposited straight into their account.

Direct Deposits are also beneficial since they can assist a parent in determining when money should be deposited into their bank account and when money should be transferred for any anticipated needs.

If they open a premium checking account, some debit cards for teens even provide free early direct deposit. This allows kids to get paid more quickly than they might with traditional direct deposit.

When you sign up for direct deposit, some debit cards can send wages up to two days faster than traditional banks.

Despite instilling in your children a feeling of delayed gratification to help them develop money management skills and long-term thinking, waiting for your hard-earned money to touch your account isn't always necessary.

After all, why should you have to wait if you deserve it?

2. Checking Account

Opening a bank account for your child or teen can teach them about financial responsibility and offer them their first experience managing money.

The nicest part about opening a checking account, or even just depositing money into one, is that it teaches future generations about saving and spending sensibly. It'll also be a terrific opportunity to teach your youngster about budgeting and how much money they should set aside.

The problem with opening a checking account for a youngster is that most banks demand parental authorization to open an account on behalf of the minor.

This implies you'll need to be present when they open the account so they can do it themselves. Furthermore, the best debit cards for kids necessitate continuing parental engagement, such as parental restrictions and activity monitoring via a mobile app.

Checking accounts are no longer the same as they were in the past. Many of the most critical services provided by most banks are now available online. As a result, many of your money transfers, payments, and other transactions no longer require you to visit a bank.

It's becoming increasingly crucial to have a digital checking account that can handle a variety of financial duties.

3. Savings Account

The greatest debit cards for kids aren't simply for teaching them how to be responsible. Because the money is pulled from the connected checking account on the card itself, and all transactions go via it, they're also a savings account in disguise.

Learning to handle this account can educate children how to save and budget money for both short- and long-term goals.

To qualify for a digital account connected to a debit card, most banks demand that you be at least 13 years old.

That is why it is critical for parents or guardians of children who will soon become teens to look into bank accounts with a linked debit card.

If your teen is interested in learning more about money and how to save and spend it properly, you should consider adding checking and savings accounts to their financial toolkit.

4. Instant Money Transfer

For parents with young children, the ability to transfer data instantly is extremely useful. When your children are too little to work or your teenagers are too preoccupied to accompany you to the bank, it is up to the parent or guardian to give them some weekly spending money from their own pocket.

Many parents use it to pay for their children's stipend or monthly tasks. The ability to make rapid transfers eliminates the need to visit a physical bank, which may be challenging for children without transportation or adults who are rushed for time.

It also allows parents to track how much money they give their children and evaluate whether they should provide more or less over time.

This feature is extremely useful for parents with active young children. Furthermore, parents who want to teach their children about financial literacy benefit from the quick transfer capability since youngsters learn how to work for their money and correlate earnings with work rather than something they receive unearned.

It's critical that children understand what it means to earn and spend money, as well as how much money they have on hand at all times. Many children's debit cards include this essential function since a rapid "reload" option allows parents to stay on top of things even when they are short on time.

5. Use Of The Mobile App

Everything has gone digital in today's modern environment. Many parents have discovered that utilizing mobile banking software makes it much easier to keep track of their children.

Teens can use a smartphone app to open their own bank account with the support of a parent, earn money to deposit into the account, and then receive access to the cash to make purchases on their own or on behalf of others.

Teens can also take control of their finances with mobile apps because they are responsible for keeping track of their spending and can see the balance of their account at all times.

Parents may set parental controls that include daily limitations, time restrictions, spending limits, and more to manage how much money is accessible for use on a mobile app, making it simple to teach youngsters about financial responsibility from a young age.

6. No Overdraft Fees

When a bank account has an inadequate balance, most prepaid debit cards can avoid overdraft fees by refusing any charges.

Because overdraft fees are usually the most expensive expenses associated with a bank account, this is a great characteristic to look for when selecting prepaid cards or debit cards linked to a bank account.

Parents can keep track of their children's spending by using expenditure controls. Kids can't spend more than a predetermined amount in any time period or location thanks to apps that allow parents to take control of the card.

That implies no overdraft fees: if the debit card for teens won't let them spend more than a certain amount (such as the remaining account balance), they won't be able to buy something that will result in an overdraft cost.

Overdraft fees aren't an issue with the Busykid Visa Prepaid Spend or Greenlight Mastercard Debit Card for Kids, for example, because you can't spend money that isn't already loaded onto the card.

Prepaid debit cards for children and teenagers are another way to minimize overdraft penalties. Prepaid debit cards, like debit cards with spending limitations set above the account balance, won't let you spend money you don't have on the card.

Overdraft costs are guarded on both sorts of cards, preventing youngsters (and you) from hefty penalties and other banking account concerns.

7. Reasonably Priced Monthly Fees

Account subscription fees are charged by many debit cards for kids in order to open and maintain an account with this financial provider.

These monthly fees have become a popular source of revenue for banks. This is how Acorns, for example, makes money.

Given the modest account balances that children and teenagers are expected to have, these monthly (or annual) fees are prevalent.

Banks normally make money by lending the money they have on deposit to borrowers. They charge the borrower a larger interest rate than they borrow from the depositor.

This gap, referred to as the net interest margin, accounts for the majority of bank profits.

Many banks, on the other hand, have pursued non-interest income in the form of one-time or monthly fees and services. Overdraft costs, account fees, account minimum balance violation fees, and other fees are only a few examples.

Many debit cards for teens choose to levy monthly fees as a way to earn money because most kids will have low account balances and will still want automated financial support for their necessities.

Thankfully, many of them provide value-added services in addition to those provided by traditional banks, making them more valuable to a parent's peace of mind.

Parental controls, spending limitations, and shared mobile app access, among other things, give parents with a compelling value proposition.

8. Parental Controls

One of the most important elements of a debit card for teenagers is parental controls. This is simple to set up and can be customized to meet the needs of any parent by allowing them to choose which notifications they want, set spending restrictions, and determine which merchants their children can visit, among other things.

Different transactions require different levels of monitoring, therefore parental controls allow for customisation, making it easier for parents who want a more detailed look at their children's spending habits.

These aren't available on a free debit card for youngsters.

Automated allowance payments, chores to do, notifications for all purchases made online and offline, and seeing expenditure reports are all possible with parental controls.

These parental controls distinguish between a traditional prepaid card and a traditional bank-issued card.

9. Kids' Reloadable Prepaid Debit Cards

A reloadable debit card for kids, also known as a prepaid debit card for kids, allows youngsters to make transactions without the fear of going overdrawn or incurring a fee for using money that isn't on their account.

Reloadable debit cards for kids only allow you to spend the money put onto them, unlike regular debit cards, which allow you to spend money held in the connected account.

On reloadable prepaid cards, you can add money to the balance at any time, allowing you to spend the money when you need it.

However, these cards can impose fees for loading a card, using it, and additional one-time or monthly costs in regular circumstances.

Although the conditions matter, the reloadable prepaid debit cards for kids outlined in this article can assess these monthly costs. Some impose a fee for reloading cash onto a reloadable card, but not for transferring monies to the card's balance by bank or debit card transfer.

10. There Is No Minimum Balance Requirement

Many parents are seeking for prepaid debit cards that don't require a minimum amount, but there's more to it than just saving money on monthly fees. You want the best of all worlds: convenience with minimal upkeep.

When you open your account, you may be charged an initial activation and issuance cost, which some issuers waive if you are a student. Acorns, for example, do not charge monthly fees to students' with .Edu email addresses.

This makes Acorns an appealing money app for teenagers about to start college or who want to learn how to invest as a teenager.

Because they often have low balances earned from chores and allowance, gifts at holidays or birthdays, or a part-time job or other online jobs for teens, the best cards for kids don't have minimum balances.

11. Money Management Features

One of the most difficult aspects of growing up is dealing with money. You have to budget your allowance, decide what all those funds mean for you in terms of buying clothes and supplies or saving up for a big purchase –

but it never seems like enough because you have so many things on your wishlist!

A bank account with a connected card can assist you by providing a budgeting tool to assist you in spending money sensibly. Many offer unique savings pods, categories, or other terms to help teenagers save money for short- and long-term financial goals.

Additionally, some money applications for kids have the opportunity to invest in stocks for kids or other teen investing objectives.

12. Interest Paid By The Parents

Some checking accounts for kids offer parent-paid interest, which can assist parents encourage their children to save money. It's a way to teach your child about the advantages and responsibilities of money management, goal-setting, and saving money to achieve those goals.

Parent-Paid Interest is an annual percentage rate that you set in the Greenlight app for your child's General Savings. Their account will collect interest on the first of every month, and all you have to do is set up a money transfer from your parent's wallet to their account.

Greenlight calculates and pays interest monthly based on your child's "Total Savings" average daily amount for the previous month. This represents the sum of general savings and savings goals.

You can pick how much interest their savings earn using Parent-Paid Interest. You can select your Parent-Paid interest to pay up to 100% if you want them to make a lot of money.

If that's too pricey, and you'd prefer pay a legitimate interest rate, you can reduce the amount to as little as 1%. It's entirely up to you!

This tool will teach your children the importance of saving money. You can show them how their savings grow as each payment is made.

13. Set Savings Objectives

The urge to set savings objectives is closely tied to parent-paid interest. Saving at a young age can instill delayed gratification, or the belief that things are more satisfying if they are earned over time.

There's also something about saving that teaches your youngster responsibility. They'll begin to comprehend what it means to budget, diversify their savings, and invest for higher returns.

Setting up savings goals, pods, or categories in these accounts helps teach your children how to save money.

These cash envelopes are a technique that entails saving every time you get paid, but in various denominations and at various periods throughout the month.

This will teach children that they cannot spend all of their money on things they desire right now since they must save for other needs later.

14. Establish Spending Boundaries

When you open a bank account as an adult, your spending limitations are likely to be set fairly high. If you have a decent credit history, you can start with as little as $500 and work your way up to $5,000 or more.

Giving children that much independence during their early years before they've had a chance to build strong money skills may not make sense.

Parents can set spending limits for their children on a daily, weekly, or monthly basis. Parents, for example, can set daily spending limitations of $25 for their children to spend on goods they desire and need.

Some people are more comfortable with cash, while others are more comfortable with cards. Cash establishes a spending restriction, which may aid in avoiding impulse purchases.

Thankfully, by allowing parents to establish spending limitations on these cards, you've created a cash-based mentality in a cashless era.

15. Have Control Over How Your Children Spend Money On The Internet

The option for parents to regulate how money is spent from their accounts is a typical feature of this new generation of kids debit cards.

This implies money spent both online and offline by narrowing down eligible merchants or even barring a select few from accepting card payments.

16. Tools For Financial Literacy

You'll want apps that can teach, enlighten, and expand your child's financial knowledge. That means bringing tools to help you spend more wisely.

It's easy to get caught up in life, and keeping track of your finances can be time-consuming. You don't have to keep track of where and how you spend your money all of the time.

As a result, many of these applications include features such as spending insights based on your past, budgeting tools for managing your money, saving categories and objectives, and more.

All of these aid in the management of money, the development of a sense of ownership, and the understanding of finances for children. Many also include financial literacy tools in the form of videos, articles, tutorials, and explainers.

Make sure you go over the material and browse the various libraries of resources to pick the most crucial subjects to present.

17. Fee-Free ATM Withdrawals Online-Only Banks Faced An Early Challenge:

How to give cash to their depositors without having a physical location where they could make ATM withdrawals without paying a fee.

Many industry experts devised a more effective alternative than traditional banks: free ATM withdrawals from a vast network of ATMs. That means you'll be reimbursed for ATM fees at tens of thousands of ATMs across the country, not just at your banks.

Check that your child's debit card includes free ATM withdrawals and the flexibility to limit how much money they can withdraw or handle on their own.

18. Rewarding Schemes

Spending money on the card may earn you rewards points that you may put toward subsequent purchases. Many of the same benefits of a credit card, such as cash back on purchases, are available with these cards.

These types of debit cards may be ideal for teaching your children how to manage money responsibly without utilizing an expensive credit line or overdrawing as they get older and have more responsibility for their own costs.

These rewards can help motivate children to save money for larger purchases, gifts, or other significant expenses.

19. Round Ups

It was invented by Acorns, and everyone other has since replicated it. Rounding up your purchase to the next dollar amount is referred to as "rounding up."

The concept behind Round Ups is that little amounts of money saved on a monthly basis would eventually add up to much larger savings in the future.

Round Ups are fun methods to teach your children about compound interest. They will save little amounts of money over time by rounding up their purchases, and with the same method, they will eventually win larger incentives.

This is an excellent savings tool for people of all ages since it teaches them how to save and invest in a simple, straightforward manner that does not overwhelm or confuse them.

These rounded-up money can be invested, and compound interest can soar to new heights.

Greenlight also offers "Round Ups" to help you make the most of your savings without having to do anything.

20. Ability To Make Charitable Contributions

Understanding the idea of giving back is also crucial for children. With the swipe of a screen and the touch of a few buttons, several of these accounts make it simple to donate to charity — with parents' permission, of course!

21. Parental And Adolescent Safety

If you misplace or steal your card, most of these digital apps allow you to pause or replace it from your app.

Having this card makes transactions with EMV chips safer and more secure than carrying cash.

For a secure banking experience, you'll also have mobile apps that need fingerprint identification, potentially facial recognition, and even multi-factor verification.

With a prepaid Mastercard or reloadable prepaid Visa card, you can keep your bank information secret.

22. FDIC Coverage

FDIC coverage, or insurance from the Federal Deposit Insurance Corporation, should be included in all bank accounts to safeguard against the loss of a depositor's funds in the event of a bank failure. When selecting a debit card for their child, this is a crucial element to consider.

23. Oversees Chores And Distributes Allowances

These debit cards for kids and teens usually come with accompanying applications that help you manage tasks and administer weekly or monthly allowances.

The apps include tools for creating, managing, and implementing a chore and allowance system, which allows you to assign and pay for all of your household responsibilities.

Make sure you check each system's functioning and see if it fulfills your requirements. Some allow for one-time, quick payouts for performed duties, while others only allow for weekly or monthly payments on a set or floating day.

24. Investing Alternatives For Compounding Returns

Some of these apps also have additional financial features, such as the ability to set up connected custodial accounts and invest in stocks.

By design, some businesses limit your child's investing selections, ensuring that your youngster can only invest in appropriate, diversified products like index funds or ETFs.

This prevents children, particularly older children, from engaging in stock trading in securities, which has resulted in various headlines for odd market activity. Consider GameStop and the stock market hysteria it sparked in early 2021, which was fueled in part by a Reddit subforum recommending the company as a strong purchase.

Others, such as Greenlight, enable individuals to invest in specific stocks, but all purchases and sells must first be approved by their parents.

Furthermore, Greenlight restricts your ability to acquire and sell companies with a market capitalization of at least $1 billion, thus avoiding penny stocks and other dangerous small-cap names.

CHAPTER NINE

FINANCIAL LESSONS DEBIT CARDS FOR CHILDREN TEACH

Debit cards may educate your children a lot more than just how to save, manage, budget, invest, give, and spend money. They can also teach them how to make money their own.

Using a debit card to interact with money necessitates opening a checking account, which stores value, and then converting the monies in the account into purchases.

As a result, learning to convert saved value from an account into a usable resource for spending and managing using a debit card necessitates responsibility.

Kids can develop financial responsibility with such power. The following are some of the most crucial lessons to learn:

1. Differentiating between wants and necessities. As children get older, they must learn to recognize the difference between wants and necessities. Any seasoned budgeting pro will tell you that it's a delicate balancing act. Many individuals propose following the 50/30/20

budgeting guideline, which requires you to consider how you will spend your funds between wants and requirements. This rule states that you should spend 50% of your money on necessities (shelter, electricity, and food), 30% on wants, and the rest in savings (20 percent).

A debit card forces you to live within your means by preventing you from using tomorrow's money to pay for today's purchases. By managing these everyday decisions with today's funds rather than tomorrow's potential profit, these card limits can help establish a deeper sense of financial literacy.

2. Being grateful for what you have. Learning to appreciate what you have is closely tied to discriminating between wants and needs. You will be more fulfilled and satisfied with your life as a result of doing so, rather than always seeking more. When you come across something you desire but can't afford with your present financial resources, you can explore for alternatives to help you make the purchase. This is something Debit will not accept. You can learn to appreciate your situation and achieve contentment by finding satisfaction with what you have.

3. Financial accountability when you add these crucial attributes together, you've instilled in your youngster a feeling of financial responsibility. These principles represent some of the most fundamental financial values that a child can learn at an early age. If done correctly and consistently, your child should be able to live a financially comfortable life.

4. Financial independence. You can start working toward financial freedom or maintain it by resisting the urge to use expensive credit and instead relying on what you already have. Getting into other people's debts goes hand in hand with achieving financial independence and being able to make life decisions that aren't exclusively based on money. Kids who can avoid getting into debt right away and never have to worry about it will have more financial peace of mind on a daily basis.

5. Maintaining financial stability. Finding financial balance is a lifelong journey for most people, packed with ups and downs and requiring ongoing attention. To put it another way, establishing financial balance is a process, not a result or a single event in your life. It's the result of a series of financial decisions that have allowed you to find the perfect financial situation for you. When

it comes to debit vs. credit, it's all about what you have now, not what you'll have tomorrow.

The Benefits and Drawbacks of Children's Debit Cards

Getting your child a debit card has various advantages, including instilling financial responsibility and teaching them about money, but it also has some drawbacks that should be considered.

Pros

•   You'll learn how to budget. Set up a weekly or monthly allowance for your child and explain that the money must last for a certain amount of time. This will assist kids in grasping the concepts of putting money down for a rainy day, making money last and better balancing wants and requirements.

•   Carry as little cash as possible. If your child needs to make a purchase while at school (say, on a field trip to the bowling alley) and there isn't an ATM nearby, this is a suitable example. You also don't want them carrying a large sum of money that could be misplaced or stolen. Federal consumer protections protect you against purchases you didn't make and from being held liable for payments made in error or with a stolen card.

- Security. You can simply deactivate their debit cards if they lose them, which will prevent any future funds from being lost. You also have EMV chips, multi-factor authentication, password-protected accounts, and parental review and approval to prevent unauthorized purchases. Even if they are not physically there with their child when making a financial decision, parents remain in control.

- Parental supervision. Checking your children's bank statements or accounts connected to a debit card or prepaid card can provide insight into their spending habits. Some cards let parents to set limits on where and how much they can spend, giving them even more control and advantages.

- Bill share with your children. Some of these debit cards come with apps that allow children to contribute to communal costs as part of their regular spending. Certain debit card apps can be used to pay for things like a cell phone bill, auto insurance payments, or sharing a Disney+ subscription.

- Parental loans for major purchases. You may share big cost purchases with your kids by having them repay them over time like a consumer line of credit, just like you can do with continuing bill sharing arrangements.

This can educate your kids how to manage loan payments for things like a new phone.

- Start saving for a rainy day. You may even work with your kids to set up and establish an emergency account for themselves because many of these financial products come with a connected app that allows you to manage how your kids' earnings are appropriated into multiple buckets (e.g., saving, spending, giving, investing). While they are still at home, this can help them develop financial security that will follow them into the real world after they leave the family nest. Establishing this need early on and in a controlled atmosphere can lead to lifelong healthy financial habits.

- Use a Custodial Roth IRA to set up a Family 401k Plan. Many parents may use these cards to manage chores and allowances, as well as to deposit wages from their children's first jobs. This means that children can contribute to Roth IRAs today to lock in low tax rates for a safe retirement later. Parents can match all money made by their children and contribute up to the amount of income produced by the child throughout the tax year, allowing the child to spend his or her earnings as they see fit. For example, if your child makes $1,500 as a lifeguard at the neighborhood pool during the summer, you may put $1,500 into a custodial Roth IRA through an app like M1 Finance and let them keep the money. You won't be able to donate the funds over their earnings together, but you might be able to split it between yourself and your child. Perhaps $750 of their money is put into the IRA, and $750 of your money is put into the IRA as well.

Cons

• Spending is simple. If you give your child a debit card that is linked to their savings account, they may spend it all. Many parents are concerned about their children's ability to spend money easily. As a result, consider setting a separate savings account for your child with limits.

• There are monthly fees. Most prepaid cards or children's debit cards come with monthly or annual fees. This might be a huge stumbling block when deciding which option is best for your children.

• Fees charged by ATMs. Make a point of avoiding cards that incur a fee every time you withdraw money.

• Fees for reloading To reload money onto a prepaid card, some cards impose a reload fee.

- Investing costs associated with custodial accounts. Although not all of the cards listed above come with an investment interface, some do. Some of these levy account fees for opening and maintaining a custodial account.

CHAPTER TEN

DEBIT CARDS FOR KIDS VS. PREPAID CARDS FOR KIDS

A basic debit card is linked to funds in a bank or credit union account. You must reload money into a prepaid debit card in order to spend the funds at a store or online.

Because the value of prepaid debit cards is tied to the card itself rather than a financial institution, they are classified as "stored-value" cards. Teens and other minors can use these debit cards as a mix of standard financial goods.

Both debit and prepaid cards offer advantages. What you desire from a card will determine which option is ideal for you. A plastic card that can be used for purchases is a debit card. It's linked to your checking account.

It can be an excellent approach to begin spending money before you open your own savings account. A debit card can also be obtained for free or for a nominal monthly cost.

Because there are no notifications, spending controls, or spending limitations with a standard bank account from a major bank or local credit union, parents can't keep a close eye on their child's spending.

While you may have account login information and check for account statements in the mail or by email, a prepaid card provides you with greater monitoring and control than traditional banks.

That's why the best debit cards for teens include these parent-friendly features, giving parents peace of mind that they can keep an eye on their children's spending patterns. They work similarly to prepaid cards in that you can't spend money you don't have.

You can limit your children's spending and prevent the card from being used at particular merchants with a prepaid card like the ones indicated above. When they use their card, you can also get fast notifications and alerts. The disadvantage, on the other hand? Fees apply to prepaid cards.

Prepaid debit cards should be considered by parents of younger children for the money controls they provide, and bank accounts should be reserved for teenagers or young adults who understand how to handle money and have the financial literacy tools they need to be self-sufficient.

Is It OK For Kids To Use Prepaid Cards?

Prepaid debit cards can be a terrific way for kids to get their feet wet in the financial world. They only allow you to spend the card's balance, but they also make it easy to transfer allowance earned through tasks or as part of a pre-determined payment schedule.

Getting youngsters started with a prepaid debit card early can help them navigate the financial system more easily as they get older, by familiarizing them with the various financial products and organizations.

Furthermore, this can assist kids in thinking about how to manage their money digitally rather than physically; yet handling physical cash early on can lead to a more tangible grasp of money later on.

Moving to a digital-based prepaid debit card after youngsters have understood how physical money works and the principles behind it could be an useful next step.

This is especially true because actual currency doesn't function as well as cards when ordering stuff online, which has become the preferred method of purchasing goods and services in recent years.

The majority of prepaid debit cards require that the youngster be at least 18 years old (or, as noted earlier, 16 or older). You can, however, get around this problem by enrolling your child as an authorized user on your existing prepaid debit card.

This gives your youngster access to a prepaid debit card that you can control and monitor, allowing you to establish spending restrictions and monitor card activities.

What To Do Before Getting A Debit Card For Kids

Consider the following factors before giving your child a debit card:

• There are monthly fees. Fees should not be related with the best debit cards for kids' online portals for reviewing expenditure or instructional tools for managing money.

• Major credit card companies. A major credit card network-backed card is one of the best for your child to use. Amex, Mastercard, Visa, and Discover are examples of credit card companies. This means that your youngster can use the card as a debit or credit card whenever he or she wants.

- Parental Controls are a great way to keep an eye on your kids. An online account that not only allows you to know where money is going and when it changes hands, but also allows you to track your child's spending patterns is a wise investment for both security and teaching them good money management skills.

- A prepaid credit card. To begin, you might want to think about getting a prepaid debit card. You can also add a new card as an authorized user to your existing accounts. As your youngster spends, the new card will access those accounts.

- Your credit score. There are several methods for loading money onto a debit card for children. For example, you may get a convertible credit card for your children and load it with whatever money they desire; however, you must pay off your debt every month to avoid interest costs. Your credit score may suffer if you do not pay off your monthly bill.

Can An 8-Year-Old, 11-Year-Old, 12-Year-Old, Or 16-Year-Old Have A Prepaid Debit Card?

Banks and credit unions have varying standards when it comes to the minimum age that an account holder must be to open an account and receive a debit card.

Some financial institutions begin at the age of eight, eleven, twelve, or even sixteen, while others offer cards specifically for parents of young children or teenagers. Parents must decide whether to use a prepaid card or a standard bank account to meet their demands.

Are Kids Too Young For Debit Cards?

We know that children as young as eight years old can obtain a debit card, but should they?

According to research, children begin creating lifelong money habits at the age of seven, so the earlier they can begin to learn about money, the better.

In fact, according to the same study, children as young as three years old begin to establish attitudes and perceptions about money as soon as they learn to count and see how their parent(s) and/or guardian(s) handle their money.

Because debit cards for kids can help them develop financial knowledge of a variety of personal finance subjects, giving them cards with parental restrictions and oversight from a young age makes sense.

This can also foster independence by allowing them to make their own decisions—with the safeguards you can provide, of course. This will give them confidence in how they behave themselves and plan for today's necessities rather than tomorrow's wants.

Debit cards may make kids feel like adults without actually being one: a win-win situation for everyone. Parents want their children to grow up, but they don't want them to leave the nest too soon.

Plus, you can trust your children (or teenagers) to make smart judgments away from home when they eventually leave.

Is A Kids' Debit Card A Good Option For Teens?

Getting a debit card for your teen can be a good idea. However, which card you choose will be determined by your child's tolerance for the environment.

Some cards provide the youngster more freedom in how he or she spends money without the approval of a parent, as long as it stays within the pre-set spending limit.

Consider a prepaid debit card for teens if you want more control over your teen's spending. If you want them to have greater flexibility, you can give them access to a teen banking app.

Are Children's Debit Cards Safe?

Yes. Because of two important qualities, children's debit cards are generally safe.

To begin with, debit cards provide significantly greater consumer protection than cash. One of the biggest benefits of using a prepaid card over cash is the liability and fraud protection provided by federal law.

Some provide purchasing protections, but challenging illegal transactions or rectifying inaccuracies on your account may be difficult.

Second, most debit cards allow you to put your card on hold or replace it if you lose it or it is stolen. Similar to the previous argument, holding a debit card is safer than carrying cash, and transactions with EMV chips are likewise safer.

Furthermore, the aforementioned cards come with mobile apps that require password protection, as well as maybe fingerprint and/or facial recognition.

Some even demand multi-factor authentication, in which you must enter a code sent to the account's associated phone to have access to your account. This ensures a safe banking experience.

Regardless, you should take all reasonable precautions to protect your personal and account information. This entails:

• Keeping your PIN number safe.

• protecting your card by putting it in a safe place.

• Not flapping it around in public

• Not revealing account information to anyone who doesn't need to know.

• Using a strong password that does not contain common terms or phrases such as "password."

• Sticking to branded bank networks when using ATMs.

• Avoiding utilizing public Wi-Fi to make transactions with your credit card, and much more.

Do Kids' And Teens' Debit Cards Collect Personal Information?

The policies of each organization differ when it comes to collecting sensitive, personal data such as names, ages, email addresses, GPS location data, transaction information, and so on.

Through their privacy rules, some companies reserve the right to share this personal information with ad and marketing partners, insurance companies, collection agencies, and a variety of other service providers.

This information may also be gathered in the future for the purpose of presenting targeted adverts and content.

For anyone above the age of 13, some of the companies included in this site require you to grant express permission or approval, which can be as simple as signing up or logging in. By creating an account, you are agreeing to the app's privacy policy.

The Children's Online Privacy Protection Act, or COPPA, makes the restrictions for children under the age of 13 more stringent. This two-decade-old legislation compels businesses to obtain "verifiable parental consent" before collecting data from kids.

The law specifies that permission must be "clearly and understandably written, full, and contain no unrelated, confusing, or contradicting materials," according to the Federal Trade Commission, which enforces it.

The method for obtaining this consent, however, is the same regardless of whether you sign up for accounts based on your age.

As a result, be cautious about the information you grant access to through your account. If you have concerns about how this information will be collected, treated, or utilized by the firm or its affiliates and partners, you should think twice about creating an account.

Giving access to your personal information has become increasingly common in today's digital-first environment.

Before you proceed with an action to open a kids debit card or any other financial product, make sure you understand your rights under COPPA (or any extensions seen at the state level, such as California's Consumer Privacy Act of 2018).

What Are Some Other Investment Accounts For Kids That I Should Look Into?

You have additional possibilities to explore if you wish to achieve certain goals with these cash.

• 529 savings schemes. Consider starting a 529 account with a business like Backer instead if you want to save money for college or other qualified educational costs.

• Roth IRAs with a custodial account. Consider a custodial Roth IRA for kids instead if you want to get a head start on saving for your child's future. This permits children with earned money to contribute at a lower tax rate than adults and receive access to more years of compounding profits. M1 Finance, for example, provides these accounts for children.

• Trust Accounts. Consider forming a trust fund if you want additional flexibility in terms of when the money flows, rather than just the age of termination or majority.

Should Children Handle Money?

Children learn best by using their hands and seeing things firsthand. That's why creating a savings account or setting a goal with a tangible piggy bank will help them understand the notion of saving.

This material aspect makes it real for them and connects them to money.

However, given enough time, you can migrate your money management to the digital realm, relying on what has become an increasingly digital environment.

You don't have to give up one completely to pursue the other. It can make financial sense to keep money in cash, as well as on your credit card and bank account.

However, we found that starting a digital account transfer from your account to their account is significantly more convenient than driving to the bank and withdrawing cash from an ATM.

What Happens If My Child's Debit Card Is Stolen?

Thankfully, FinTech apps linked to your cards make locking your cards a breeze, preventing any potential fraudulent behavior from someone who discovers the card before you do.

You have the option of locking the card, canceling it, and ordering a new one. Some apps charge for this service, while others provide it for free.

Fortunately, losing a card has no consequence if you act quickly enough. It's not like losing a bunch of cash, which can't be replaced. As a result, cards make money handling easier, safer, and more secure.

Is It Possible For Kids To Get Their Own (Custom) Debit Cards?

Kids can acquire a debit card with their name and a picture of their choice on it. Kids and teens will be more likely to engage with their cards and the responsibilities they represent if this is allowed.

Furthermore, the one-of-a-kind card may make individuals less likely to misplace or lose their card, as well as keep track of the balance. They'll have something they can be proud of that reflects their individual flair.

When users use the card, customers see either their bank account balance or a message reminding them of their spending limits. They may chat to their parents about how to appropriately use their personalised card and save money for important purchases like a new phone, laptop, or even college tuition.

What Documents Are Required To Open A Debit Card For Children And Teenagers?

The federal government compels these card businesses to "know" their clients via a process known as "Know Your Customer," or KYC, because they are financial service organizations.

This commonly used computerized validation of identity and information complies with the US Patriot Act of 2001's regulatory obligations.

This method checks your name, address, and date of birth against a public records database, such as one provided by one of the three major credit reporting bureaus, at the time of account sign-up.

While this check verifies your information to ensure you are who you say you are, it is not a credit check, so neither you nor your child's credit scores will be harmed.

You may receive notice that a financial service has verified your address, but this will not affect your credit score.

If you've only been able to meet a partial match based on public records databases, you may need to upload extra information depending on how long you've resided at your present address. Uploading a copy of your driver's license or state-issued identification may be required.

These documents should match the information you supply in your first account application to these debit card providers.

It can take anywhere from 24 to 72 hours for this information to be verified once you've uploaded it. You should receive an email from the service provider informing you whether you passed, allowing you to open the account.

Is It Possible To Make Contactless Payments With A Teen Debit Card?

Many card providers have advanced their cardholders' capacity to use contactless payments technology as a result of COVID-19.

This covers teen and child debit cards. Many of the cards mentioned in this article can be used in stores to make contactless payments and transactions.

However, before making your first contactless transaction, you may need to test the card's operation using the classic chip and PIN method.

You may be able to use the card contactlessly for subsequent purchases beyond this point, though there may be maximum per transaction limits.

Contact your provider or check the terms of service for further information about contactless payments and payment maximums.

CHAPTER ELEVEN

CONCLUSION

When Opening A Brokerage Account For Your Child, These Are The Things To Look For

Kids can invest, too, and it's never too early to start. You can help your children choose investments by opening a custodial brokerage account for them.

Investing isn't just for adults: opening a custodial brokerage account with your children can be a terrific way to teach them about money and the importance of investment development.

A lengthy time horizon is one of the most important aspects of successful investing, and youngsters have plenty of it. They're likely to receive a substantial return on their initial investment if they're willing to leave their money invested for several years. Seeing their money increase as an adult can motivate them to be better savers and investors when it matters most.

Here are some things to think about when it comes to investing for kids, such as the best investments and how to choose and set up your child's first brokerage account. To avoid any misunderstandings, this sort of account is also known as a custodial account or a UGMA/UTMA account.

Are you ready to start your child on the path to financial independence? To assist your child with getting started, follow this step-by-step guide.

Choose An Account Type
To get your kids started investing, you'll need to figure out which account is ideal for them. This decision is mostly based on whether or not they have a source of income.

• If your child does not have taxable income or earnings, you can open custodial brokerage accounts for them under the Uniform Gift to Minors Act or Uniform Transfer to Minors Act (UGMA/UTMA). Although the account will be in your name at first, after your child reaches the age of 18 or 21, depending on state rules, he or she will be able to assume full management of it. (For additional information on UTMA and UGMA accounts, click here.)

• If your child earns taxable earnings or income: You can assist your children in opening a custodial IRA if they are older and have earned income. A Roth IRA, in particular, is a great option for kids: Your child's contributions to the account will grow tax-free. The gains from the investments can be used for a number of things, including retirement, a first home, and school. These contributions are withdrawable whenever you choose.

Select The Appropriate Broker

You'll need to choose a broker first, regardless of which form of brokerage account you decide to open for your children. There are no account fees and no minimum initial contribution with the finest investment accounts for kids. This allows your children to begin investing with a tiny sum of money.

Find a broker online with a low investment requirement and no account fees.

Take into account the costs of the investments your child intends to make. For example, if your child wants to practice stock trading, make sure the broker has low or no trade commissions. Look for brokers who have a big range of low-cost index funds if your kids merely want their money to grow without them having to do anything.

Many brokers offer instructional content, such as online investment seminars and even practice trading accounts, if you're looking for a brokerage account to teach your kids about investing.

Open The Account

In approximately 15 minutes, you can open a custodial account for your child — both a conventional brokerage account and a Roth IRA — with most brokers; the entire process is performed online.

Make sure you have all of the relevant information on hand to expedite the process. You and your child's Social Security numbers, as well as dates of birth and contact information, will almost certainly be requested by the broker. You'll almost certainly be asked for your work details, and you should be prepared to link another bank or brokerage account so that money may be transferred to the new account.

Assist Your Child In Deciding What To Buy

The real fun begins once the custodial account is opened and funded: investing the money.

Your children will be able to invest in individual stocks, mutual funds, index funds, and exchange-traded funds through their brokerage account.

We recommend a two-pronged approach to get your kids interested in investing:

1. Assist them in selecting one or two specific stocks. Concentrate on well-known companies — even owning a small percentage of well-known businesses can pique their interest in investing.

2. Use index funds to make up the rest of your portfolio. We encourage bypassing further shares of specific stocks when your youngster adds money to the investment account and instead focuses on low-cost index funds or ETFs. These funds give the portfolio the much-needed diversification it needs by pooling hundreds of stocks into a single investment. Your youngster will be able to invest in a variety of companies in one transaction.

Make a routine of examining their gains and losses every few days after they've chosen and purchased their investments, and comparing little swings to greater long-term changes. This will generate debate and encourage children to become better informed investors in the future. This is also a good moment to discuss the advantages of opening many investing accounts for different goals.

Good luck!

www.ingramcontent.com/pod-product-compliance
Lightning Source LLC
Chambersburg PA
CBHW071504220526
45472CB00003B/907